INTRODUCTION

Since the pages of this book was digitized from a very old original, the pages here may look a little funny at times. Rest assured we did our best to format the original book into modern form as best allowed by the current processes available.

Ross Brown

Introduction and Cover Art Copyright 2009 -
All rights reserved.
SoHoBooks
ISBN 1441404163

For regular updates on new reprint editions of
vintage cookbooks,
vintage cocktail books,
vintage bar books
vintage drink books and
vintage wine books
please visit

www.HistoricCookbooks.com

*Give us a vote and we will cook
The better for a wide outlook*

WASHINGTON WOMEN'S COOK BOOK

PUBLISHED BY
THE WASHINGTON EQUAL SUFFRAGE
ASSOCIATION

COMPILED BY
LINDA DEZIAH JENNINGS

1909:
TRADE REGISTER PRINT
SEATTLE, WASH.

STATE EXECUTIVE BOARD

President, MRS. EMMA SMITH DEVOE,
Thorp

Vice-Presidents

MRS. MAY ARKWRIGHT HUTTON
Hutton Bldg., Spokane

MRS. JENNIE JEWETT, White Salmon

MISS ELLEN GRAHAM, Avon

Cor. Secretary, MRS. ELLEN S. LECKENBY
Brighton Beach

Rec. Secy., MRS. ANNA E. GOODWIN, Columbia

Press, Eastern Washington,
MRS. M. LA REINE BAKER
"The Spokane," Spokane

Treasurer, DR. CORA SMITH EATON
1629 14th Avenue

Auditors

ANNA W. SCOTT, D. O., West Seattle

MISS BERNICE SAPP, Olympia

Historian, MRS. BESSIE I. SAVAGE
212 23rd Avenue North, Seattle

Member of National Executive Committee
MISS ADELLA M. PARKER
419 Boylston Avenue North, Seattle

Trustees

MRS. B. B. LORD, Olympia
DR. SARAH KENDALL, 477 Arcade, Seattle
MRS. GEORGE B. SMITH, Anacortes

Chairmen of Standing Committees, State Members
MRS. ELIZABETH PALMER SPINNING, Puyallup

Letter Writers, MRS. LUCIE F. ISAACS, Walla Walla

Headquarters, MRS. C. M. MILLER
1902 E. Thomas St., Seattle

Literature, MRS. E. M. WARDALL
West Seattle

Legislation, MRS. HOMER M. HILL
1227 Main St., Seattle

Labor Unions, DR. LUEMA G. JOHNSON
1014 Sixth Ave., Tacoma

Publication, MISS LINDA JENNINGS
La Conner

House-to-House Canvass,
MRS. EDITH DE L. JARMUTH
32 Westminster Apartments
9th Ave. and Marion St., Seattle

Educational, MRS. MARGARET HEYES HALL
Vancouver

Superintendent of Parlor Meetings
MRS. NELLIE M. RENINGER

The Bulletin
MISS MAY GRINNELL, Editor
499 Arcade, Seattle

MISS MARGARET W. BAYNE, Manager
Kirkland

PREFACE.

A preface to a compilation of cooking recipes may seem to many to be quite unnecessary, but let us look deeper for a moment and we will see that modern cooking represents the evolution of civilized life. Students of the human race declare that it was woman who first discovered how to build a fire; these learned ones are divided in opinion as to whether she was actuated by a desire to make more palatable the food for her offspring, or to keep it warm. Nevertheless, with the ability to make a fire began cookery. The inventive genius of those first months made up a cook-book, limited indeed, yet passed on from mother to daughter as the best product of the wisdom of their times.

We present you these recipes, product of the civilization of our times. In them are represented science, art and the human desire to produce things beautiful.

Are not our desserts and salads things of beauty and the joy of a moment?

Home, a smiling woman, and a good dinner—does not the heart of man yearn toward this trio at evening time? In the best interests of all concerned, we offer you this little book.

ACKNOWLEDGMENT AND EXPLANATION.

We wish that every person who has contributed recipes for the compiling of this cook-book would take this as a personal letter of thanks. It may be possible that your recipe was not used; so many duplicates of certain things were sent in that it was not possible to use them all.

Then again, it was not definitely decided that the recipes were to be signed, until much work had been done; so many good recipes had been received to which it was impossible for us to obtain signatures.

This is the Washington Women's Cook-Book, and we have tried hard that all might be represented by name. For obvious reasons, that had been received to which it was impossible for us to obtain signa-
in it, as a means of good cooking and sure voting.

Dedication

TO the first woman who realized that half of the human race were not getting a square deal, and who had the courage to voice a protest; and also to the long line of women from that day unto this, who saw clearly, thought strongly, and braved misrepresentation, ridicule, calumny and social ostracism, to bring about that millennial day when humanity shall know the blessedness of dwelling together as equals.

To all those valiant and undaunted soldiers of progress we dedicate our labors in compiling this volume.

COPYRIGHTED 1908
THE WASHINGTON EQUAL SUFFRAGE ASSOCIATION
ALL RIGHTS RESERVED

Soups

"The man who neglects to vote shows small interest in the welfare of his country and is not a good citizen. What shall we say of the patriotism of the woman who would not vote if she could?"

So many good soups are found in other departments of this book that we have not considered many kinds here.

The soups in the department, "Food for the Sick," are especially fine.

Brown Soup Stock.

Seven pounds of beef, three quarts of cold water, six pepper corns, six cloves, one bay leaf, one teaspoon of thyme, one sprig of parsley, two cups of chopped vegetables, two teaspoons of salt. Cut the meat in one inch cubes. put two-thirds of it in a kettle with three quarts of cold water, let stand for an hour, put the one-third of meat in a skillet with some of the trimmings and marrow from the bones, brown and add to the stock. Let it simmer four or five hours, then add the seasonings and vegetables and simmer one hour, then strain. When cold the grease will rise to the top and form a thick cake. This you take off and the stock forms a jelly-like substance.

White Soup Stock.

Cut a large grown chicken into pieces and cover with cold water. Add one teaspoon of salt and let simmer for several hours, or until perfectly cooked. Then add one-fourth cup of chopped celery, one blade of parsley, a small onion, a tiny bit of mace, and let it simmer one-half hour longer. Strain and it is ready for use.—From "What to Cook and How to Cook It."

Tomato Soup.

One pint of strained tomatoes, one pint of rich soup stock, a piece of bay leaf no larger than a silver quarter, two cloves, one-half teaspoon each of paprika, salt and soda, one tablespoon each of sugar, chopped onion (partly fried), flour and butter.

Put all ingredients together, omitting butter and flour,

simmer for half an hour, then strain. Rub flour and butter together until smooth and thicken the soup.

If this is made exactly as the recipe is given it will be found to be a very excellent soup.

MRS. D. O'LEARY, Seattle.

Tomato Broth.

Cook tomatoes until tender, or use canned tomatoes, mash and strain to remove seeds, return to the fire and season with salt, very little red pepper or paprika and a small piece of butter. If too thick add a little hot water.

MRS. GEORGE SMITH, Anacortes.

Creole Celery Soup.

Take shank of beef, boil and skim, cut into small pieces a large bunch of celery, boil in the broth until tender, add seasoning and cup rich cream.

Chicken Cream Tomato Soup.

One quart chicken stock, one can tomatoes strained, season to taste, one half cup cream added last.

Bean Soup.

Brown beans boiled until very soft, put through a colander, add about a pint, or more if desired, to one quart of strained meat stock. Season with pepper and salt and a pinch of cayenne. Just before serving add juice of one lemon, and two hard boiled eggs chopped very fine.

MRS. LOLA FOWLER, Stanwood.

Tomato Soup.

Put on to heat one quart of good rich milk; then in another pan one can of tomatoes, strain tomatoes through seive or colander, when tomatoes come to a boil put one even teaspoon of soda in them. A lump of butter may be put in the milk if it is not rich, season with pepper and salt. Mix tomatoes and milk just before serving.

MRS. ANDREW OSBERG, LaConner.

Cheese Soup.

Use clear beef stock strained and just as it is served add to each dish a tablespoon of grated cheese. Very fine.

MRS. D. O'LEARY, Seattle.

Cream Potato Soup.

For six persons. Put in a double boiler one quart milk, add two medium sized potatoes already cooked well done in one pint of water, also a small onion fried light brown in two level tablespoons of butter, salt and pepper. Thicken if desired with one teaspoon flour stirred smooth in cold water. Let come to boiling point.

MRS. NELLIE M. RININGER, Seattle.

Grapenuts Broth.

Half cup grapenuts put to soak in pint of rich cold milk. Heat very slowly to avoid curdling; almost to boiling point. When thoroughly softened, strain and add pinch of salt.

MISS GERTRUDE WALLACE, Stanwood.

Tomato.

Take one can of tomatoes, one quart of water, one medium sized onion. Cook thoroughly. Add pinch of soda, then stir in the following sauce: One pint milk, large piece of butter, one tablespoon flour.

Heat the butter, stir in the flour, add salt and pepper to taste.

Heat the milk and add to this. Then stir this into the tomato when it is below boiling point.

If milk is not available, add more water to the tomato and thicken with spaghetti broken up fine, and season.

Vegetable.

Chop two large potatoes, one onion, one small cabbage, one turnip.

Place butter size of egg in kettle and heat. Pour in the chopped vegetables and stir well. Add two quarts of hot water, boil one hour and season to taste.

Potato.

Four potatoes cut into dice; one large onion, chopped; cover with water and cook until tender. Add one quart of milk, tablespoon butter, pepper and salt to taste. Bring to a boil and serve.

Cream of Celery.

Cut up one bunch of celery into one quart of water. Boil until tender and thicken with same sauce used in the tomato soup.

Corn.

Take one can of corn, cook until well done, add pint of rich milk, one tablespoon of butter, pepper and salt to taste. If onion flavor is liked, a few slices may be added.

Fish and Shell Fish

"It is cheap wit that finds it so amusing that women should vote."—RALPH WALDO EMERSON.

Clam Chowder.

Twenty clams, two medium sized potatoes, one large onion chopped fine, two well-beaten eggs, six crackers rolled fine; cut potatoes into small pieces; mix, season and add strained juice, chopped clams to be added after potatoes are done.

It is improved by the addition of half cup rich cream.

Excellent Clam Soup.

Two quarts of clams in the shell or one quart of opened clams. If in the shell cover with water and let stand over night or several hours to spit sand, then wash the shells with small brush, rinsing well to remove sand. Then put into a baking pan or steamer, cook twenty minutes. Take enough milk for the number of persons to be served—this should be enough clams for soup for six people—heat in granite dish, add good sized piece of butter, pepper, and two or three crackers rolled fine. Take the clams from the shell, put into the milk, also the juice in the baking pan. If shelled clams are used, they should be cut in pieces and stewed ten minutes in a little water. The milk and liquor to be heated separately, as the milk will curdle if cooked together. Put together just before serving.

MRS. JENNIE G. CLEGG, Spokane.

Clam Chowder.

One-half cup chopped ham or bacon, put in large kettle to fry; add to this three onions chopped fine; when browned slightly add three quarts boiling water. Add to the above six medium sized potatoes cut in dice, cook twenty minutes. Now add one can minced clams or one teacup of fresh clams chopped fine. Last of all add one cup rolled crackers and one quart milk, let come to a boil, season and serve hot.

MRS. L. M. HALL, Puyallup.

Clam Fritters.

Clean a half dozen large clams, remove heads, chop fine, add one beaten egg to a tablespoon of milk and a little flour. Season with salt and pepper then fry in a skillet in form of pancakes.

MRS. ANDREW OSBERG, LaConner.

Clam Bouillon.

To one small can of clam chowder add three cups of boiling water, two cups milk, one cup strained tomatoes; heat tomatoes first in separate dish; add a little soda and one dessert spoonful of flour mixed with water. Cook three minutes and strain through wire strainer.

Serve in bouillon cups with whipped cream.

MRS. H. M. CHITTENDEN, Seattle.

Creamed Clams.

Scald the clams in their own liquor, chop them fine and measure. To each cupful of chopped clams add one cupful of thick cream sauce.

For one cupful of sauce, melt one tablespoon of butter, stir in one tablespoon of flour, cook but do not brown it; then add slowly one-half cup of clam liquor and one-half cup of milk or cream; season with pepper and salt.

Let it cook until a smooth thick cream, stirring all the time. Add the clams just before serving. Pour over small pieces of toast.

MRS. ANNA M. COMBES, Elma.

Clam Fritters.

One dozen clams chopped fine; add the liquor from the clams to a batter made of one pint of milk, six tablespoons of flour, six eggs well beaten, two tablespoons of melted butter a little salt and pepper. Drop from a spoon into hot oil or lard; fry a light brown. Or dip the whole clam into the batter and fry as you do oysters. Serve very hot.

MRS. ANNA M. COMBES, Elma.

Scalloped Oysters.

One quart of fresh oysters, eight soda crackers rolled fine, put in layers in a baking pan, sprinkle with pepper and salt. Save the liquor and add with enough milk to cover just before putting them in the oven. Put rolled crackers with bits of butter on top. Bake three-quarters of an hour.

MERTON M'KEE, Avon.

Oysters Cocktails.

Use Olympia oysters; fill cocktail glass one-third full of drained oyster, finish filling with tomato catsup, place a drop of tobasco sauce in each and a squeeze of lemon; season, and serve with sliced lemon and wafers.

Oyster Cocktails.

Drain Olympia oysters, drench with boiling water, pouring off instantly; set away on ice a few minutes to chill. This is to prevent the sliminess that some persons so object to. Fill the cocktail glass a little less than half full of oysters; finish the glass with tomato catsup in which has been put three drops of tobasco sauce (three drops for the entire serving) and a squeeze of lemon to each glass.

MRS. G. F. ZIMMERMAN, Seattle.

Oyster Omelet.

Beat the yolks of six eggs into a teacup of milk and add a cup and a half of small oysters drained; then add the whites of the eggs beaten stiff. Fry in hot butter and do not stir while cooking. Slip a knife around the edges, that the center may cook equally.

MRS. ANNA M. COMBES, Elma.

Ludt Fish.

(A Swedish Christmas Dainty.)

Three dried unsalted codfish, soak in water three days in a cool place. Drain off the water, then dissolve four heaping teaspoons of soda in two gallons of water, soak the fish in this for three days. Drain off water and soak in fresh water over night, or a few hours. Drain off water again, put the fish in boiling water and cook ten minutes.

Serve with cream or milk gravy or melted butter. It is also nice either cold or hot without dressing.

MRS. THILDA ANDERSON, Avon.

Baked Salmon.

Take small salmon, opened underneath and fill with

bread dressing as you would fowl (it will not be necessary to sew up the fish). Put in long baking pan, sprinkle with pepper and salt and dot with whole allspice. Bake and serve with the following sauce:

Sauce.

One cup of liquor where fish has been baked, and one cup of milk or cream, thickened with one tablespoon flour. Season with pepper and salt.

MISS EMMA SWANSON.

Baked Salmon—Spanish.

Remove skin from the fish and cut in thick slices, put in dripping pan and season well, then on top of each slice place a spoonful of chopped onion. Bake until done, then put a spoonful of tomato on each slice and return to the oven just long enough to heat the tomato. Serve with the following sauce:

Sauce.

Cook one chopped onion in a little butter, strain half a can of tomatoes into it, season well and thicken slightly.

Fried Smelt.

Remove the intestines, wash and drain; roll in salted flour and fry very quickly in hot, deep fat to a rich brown.

Be sure to have plenty of fat; have it hot and fry quickly if you would have the fish tender.

Boiled Fish.

Perhaps fish is best boiled by steam. Place the fish on clean cloth in the steamer and steam until done. By this method it will not go to pieces and may be served whole.

Serve with drawn butter sauce.

Fish Turbot.

Make dressing of one pint milk and one tablespoon flour, cool and add two eggs well beaten and one-half cup butter. Take and cool fish, put in layers of fish and dressing alternately in a buttered baking dish.

Cover the top with rolled bread crumbs and bake twenty minutes.

MRS. CLARA SAUERS, Aberdeen.

Clams

Contributed by Mrs. Bessie I. Savage.

Of the seven or eight varieties of clams found on Puget Sound, with which I am familiar, all but one (the boring clam) are good to eat and if properly prepared furnish the best of food. Where possible see that your clams are from beaches remote from large cities. Get them in the shells and see that all are alive. If the shells are not closed or do not close tightly, reject them. As soon as obtained put in clean water to which has been added one tablespoon of salt to each gallon. Let stand at least six hours. If desired to keep longer than twelve hours, the water should be changed every day and corn meal sprinkled on top of water as soon as clams are put in.

For steaming and baking the shells should be thoroughly washed with a small brush.

If the clams are hard to open pour boiling water on them.

For frying use the large butter clam. For steaming or baking use only the little neck or cockle clam.

Steamed Clams.

Choose small to medium sized Little Necks. Wash, put in a kettle with half a teacupful of water to a five-pound lard bucketful of clams, cover tightly, boil from fifteen to twenty minutes. Serve hot. (Save the liquor for boullion, etc.)

Baked Clams.

Prepare as for boiling, put in a large bread pan, bake in hot oven until shells open.

Clam Puree.

Take one pint of the liquor from steamed or baked clams, add one pint of water, butter the size of an egg, pepper and salt to taste, a little nutmeg. Boil, thicken to the consistency of cream. When ready to serve add one pint of hot milk and serve immediately.

Clams on Toast.

Drain lightly one pint of shelled Little Neck (Butter Clams will not do). Add half a teacup of water. Let this come to a boil, thicken to the consistency of cream, add a tablespoon of butter, season with salt, pepper and nutmeg Serve on toast.

Fried Clams.

Choose large white Butter Clams. Open, cut out and reject the necks. Drain, dip in beaten egg, roll in cracker crumbs or farina. Fry in deep fat (as doughnuts).

Clam Croquettes.

Chop and drain a pint of shelled clams. Put in frying pan with a tablespoon of butter and let cook two or three minutes. Add half as much bread crumbs and a beaten egg. Season with salt and pepper. Roll and fry in hot deep fat.

Scrambled Clams With Eggs.

One-half pint of shelled small Little Necks (or chopped large ones). Put in a frying pan with a tablespoon of butter, and when they have cooked two minutes or until edges curl, add three eggs. Stir frequently, and serve on toast.

Pan Roast a la Doane.

Make a sauce as follows: One tablespoon of butter, melt, stir in two tablespoons of flour, one teacup of boiling water, two tablespoons of tomato juice, one-half teaspoon of curry powder, salt, pepper and nutmeg to taste.

Let cook two minutes, add clams, cook three minutes. Serve on buttered toast.

Clam Fritters.

Prepare a batter as for fruit fritters, stir in well drained Little Necks. Fry in hot, deep fat.

Clam Pie.

Prepare clams as for creamed clams. Line the sides of a sauce pan (not the bottom) with pastry as for chicken pie, fill with clams prepared as for creamed clams, cover with crust. Bake.

Clam Omelet.

Prepare eggs as for plain omelet. Just before the eggs set pour on half a pint of well drained Little Necks, to a three egg omelet. Fold and serve hot.

'Scalloped Clams.

Prepare as for creamed clams. To one pint of clams add one pint of bread crumbs soaked in milk. Dot the top with small bits of butter, brown in oven and serve hot.

Very small Little Necks make excellent cocktails prepared as oysters.

Meats

"There is no freedom on earth nor in any star for those who deny freedom to others."

Roast Beef.

In thinking of meats, perhaps roast beef comes first to our minds. No other meat is so nutritious if properly cooked.

The outside must be seared at once to keep in the juices. To do this either put on grate of a very hot oven or by pressing every side down on a hot pan on top of the range.

What is known as rib roasts are the best, and one can hardly get the best results with a roast under ten or twelve pounds.

Fillet Roast of Beef.

Trim, wipe the fillet with a damp cloth and skewer into shape. Lard the meat and dredge with flour, salt and pepper, place on rack in roasting oven and sear over quickly. When nicely browned reduce the heat and continue the roasting until the meat is tender.

Serve with mushroom sauce.

MRS. BERT ESTERBROOK, Bellingham.

Flank Steak.

Fry in butter until brown a flank steak, salt, pepper, put in roasting pan, pour over the butter; cover with sliced onions, heap on some tomatoes and season. Bake one and one-half hours, add water while cooking to make gravy. This is good.

MRS. ED. NEWENGER, Bellingham.

Favorite Roast Turkey.

For dressing take first joint of wings, part of neck, heart, liver and gizzard, boil soft. When nearly done add five potatoes. When all are cooked remove bones and chop; season with salt, pepper and butter. Soak nearly a small loaf of bread in the broth and mix in this dressing. Now stuff the turkey and sew up. Tie the legs together and fasten legs and wings close to body. Put enough water in the roaster to baste with; salt the turkey; turn it over often while it roasts. Bake fifteen minutes to the pound.

W. J. CROFT, Avon.

Sheep's Tongues Spanish.

Six sheep's tongues or three calves tongues. Boil the tongues about two hours. Make a sauce of one tablespoon of butter, two of olive oil, four small onions, fry them in the oil and butter, add two large tablespoons flour, clove of garlic and quart of tomatoes strained; add water the tongues were boiled in; cook slowly and add carrots and celery to taste. Pour sauce over tongues and serve hot.

MRS. CARRIE OAKLEY, Anacortes.

Veal Loaf.

One and one-half pounds veal, one-half pound lean pork, chopped very fine. Two eggs well beaten, three crackers rolled to powder. One-half cup milk, season with salt and pepper to taste. Mix all well together, form into a loaf, sprinkle the top with dry bread crumbs or powdered crackers and little bits of butter. Put in a pan with a little water and bake for an hour, occasionally adding a little water if the pan gets dry.

MRS. ANNA COMBES, Elma.

Cabbage Rolls.

Take as many whole leaves from a good cabbage head as you need. Put in each leaf a piece of round steak or hamburger steak, sprinkle with salt, pepper, ginger and cloves. Roll tie strings around to keep in shape, boil in broth or salted water for one hour. Pull off the strings and serve with melted butter.

MRS. O. OFFERDAHL.

Beef Loaf.

One and one-half pounds chopped beef, three well beaten eggs, one cup powdered crackers, one cup boiling water, salt and pepper to taste. Cover with boiling water and cook one and one-half hours.

MARIA HAYS M'HENRY, Olympia.

Baked Liver.

Have in reserve some good stock made from the shin of the beef, or bouillon made from Armour's Extract. Ten cents' worth calves liver, some slices of bacon, onions and stale bread. Take a medium sized individual baking pan. Lay in the bottom some thin slices of bacon, cover these with slices of liver, slice some onions over this, add salt and pepper and cover with thin slices of stale bread. Repeat this until the pan is nearly full. Pour over the soup stock to nearly cover, putting slices of bread on top cover. Bake thirty or forty minutes.

Remove cover, brown bread nicely and serve.

MRS. JENNIE G. CLEGG, Spokane.

Veal Cutlets.

W. S. C. Domestic Science Dept.

Use slices of veal from leg, cut at least one-half inch thick, wipe and remove bone, skin, cut in small pieces. For serving fasten small pieces together with clean tooth picks. Sprinkle with salt, pepper; dip in flour, then in beaten egg and cracker crumbs or bread. Cook in hot fat until well browned on both sides, then place in well seasoned brown gravy. Allow to simmer on back of range at least one hour.

Sauce or Gravy for Above.

Melt three tablespoons butter, add three tablespoons flour, stir until smooth, then add hot worcestershire gradually and last, the seasoning.

Boil five minutes, one-half cup tomatoes may be added.

Boneless Birds.

Pound and cut good fresh round steak into three inch squares. Put small piece of bacon in each square; sprinkle with salt and pepper, ginger and cloves. Roll and tie a string around each square, so it gets the shape of a bird; roll in flour and brown in butter. Pour over enough water to cover the birds. Let boil for one hour.

MRS. O. OFFERDAHL, Seattle.

Veal Stew.

Two pounds of veal cut in small pieces; cover with boiling water and cook until half done; then season with salt and paprika (sweet red pepper), add two green onions cut fine, four medium sized carrots cut in cubes, and one and one-half cups of green peas. When cooked add one pint of milk, thicken with two spoons of flour.

MRS. D. O'LEARY, Seattle.

Fried Chicken.

Select chicken weighing about two and one-half pounds. Plymouth Rocks are the best.

Wash and wipe well, cutting each chicken into four pieces, sprinkle with salt and cayenne pepper mixed, roll in flour, or in powdered cracker or bread crumbs; fry one-half hour in lard and butter. Cover while cooking with perforated cover.

MRS. H. M. CHITTENDEN, Seattle.

Chicken with Baked Dumplings.

Cut the chicken into pieces and stew until tender, when done put into a deep baking pan. If there is not enough liquor to nearly cover the chicken, add water and thicken to make a nice gravy, having previously seasoned well. Make a rich baking powder biscuit dough, cut out the biscuits and place on top of the chicken. Bake just long enough to cook the biscuits nicely. By many this is much preferred to boiled dumplings.

MRS. R. H. BALL, LaConner.

Smothered Chicken.

Cut up chicken as to fry, put in deep pan; season with salt, pepper and lumps of butter. Over this sift flour thickly; cover with water. Bake three hours.

MRS. E. S. BROWN, Bellingham.

Luncheon Chicken.

Cook a good fat chicken until very well done, keeping nearly covered with water. Remove chicken from broth and pick from bones. Make dressing as to stuff chicken which is roasted in oven.

Put in a baking dish, alternate layers of chicken and dressing. Pour over it the broth in which the chicken was cooked.

Just before serving put in the oven. Serve very hot.

Use plenty of pepper and salt and a slice of lemon when stewing the chicken. This will serve twelve persons.

MRS. G. F. ZIMMERMAN, Seattle.

Chicken Pie.

A fat hen is necessary for a good chicken pie. Cut up the chicken and place in enough boiling water to cover, and boil until tender. When cooked if the water has boiled away add enough so that the chicken will be more than covered with liquor. Thicken this to make a nice gravy. Line the sides of the baking dish with rich biscuit dough; put in the chicken and gravy and cover with crust. Bake in a moderate oven until the crust is rich brown.

MRS. A. M. CURRIER, LaConner.

Baked Chicken (Southern Style).

Take young spring chicken, after being dressed, cut open down the back, lay flat and whole in baking pan and cover with strips of bacon. Bake until tender and serve on platter with garnish of parsley. Make a gravy of the chopped giblets flavored with dried celery leaves.

MRS. HELEN J. BERRY, Bellingham.

Boiled Leg of Lamb—Caper Sauce.

Boil the leg of lamp until very tender, then take the water in which it was boiled as the foundation of the sauce. There should be at least a pint of the stock; thicken with two tablespoons of flour, season with pepper and salt, and add two tablespoons of pickled capers. Let the sauce stand fifteen minutes before using that the sauce may be well seasoned with the capers.

MRS. D. O'LEARY. Seattle.

Veal Stew.

Cut veal in small pieces and stew, when cooked pour in an equal amount of creamy milk, thicken, add a spoonful of butter; serve on platter and garnish with green peas.

MRS. HELEN J. BERRY, Bellingham.

Dumplings for Meat.

Two cups and a half of flour, sift with two teaspoons of baking powder, one teaspoon of salt, one cup of water. This should make a stiff dough to be stirred with a spoon; when the meat is done, drop the batter into the kettle where the meat is cooking, a spoonful at a time, cover closely and boil for twenty minutes.

Picnic Meat.

Buy a quantity of cheap meat (beef) salt and boil until it begins to drop from the bones. While hot chop the meat coarsely; season with sage and pepper, or some prefer chopped onion. After mixing pack in a jar; cover with a plate and sink it down with a stone or some other weight. Let sand over night, then cut in slices.

This is good any time when cold meat is wanted.

Other kinds of meat may be used.

MRS. RENA FORREST, Anacortes.

Oyster-Chestnut Dressing (For Fowl).

Three cups bread crumbs, one and one-half cups chestnuts, chopped fine (first boil and blanch), two dozen small oysters, one-half cup melted butter, one small onion, one tablespoon minced parsley, or teaspoon of dry celery leaves.

This is very good indeed, and unusually rich. Use either chestnuts or oysters leaving out the other, is fine.

MRS. HELEN J. BERRY, Bellingham.

Dressing for Fowl or Meat.

Slice one large onion and boil about half done; crumble coarsely to the amount required; moisten with hot water and add a cup or more of the juice from the roast (in the case of fowl where the dressing is put into the uncooked fowl this will be impossible), add the onion and season with pepper and salt. Have very moist.

MISS MADGE JENNING, LaConner.

Meat and Fish Sauce

Tartar Sauce.

One tablespoon chopped parsley, one teaspoon mustard (dry mustard mixed with cold water), one minced onion, one teaspoon chopped capers, dash of cayenne, one-half pint salad dressing, Durkee's preferred. Nice with all kinds of fried fish, oysters or meat croquettes.

MRS. HELEN BERRY, Bellingham.

Cream Sauce.

One cup of milk or cream, thickened with one tablespoon of butter rubbed with one tablespoon of flour. Thin this with one cup of stock. This is especially fine for baked fish. In this case be sure to use a cup of the juice where the fish is baked to thin the sauce. Many seasonings may be added, such as chopped parsley, mushrooms or oysters, when one wants to serve a fancy dish.

MISS EMMA SWANSON.

Fish Sauce.

One and one-half cups of water, half cup butter, thicken with a rounded teaspoon of cornstarch, add tablespoon lemon juice, dash of paprika. Two well beaten eggs added when partly cooled.

MRS. D. O'LEARY, Seattle.

Tomato Sauce (For Boiled Tongue).

One can tomatoes heated and strained, two scant tablespoons sago soaked in cold water, one heaping tablespoon sugar, one teaspoon each of salt. Worcestershire sauce, and walnut ketchup, five drops mapeline, a little paprika, or a trifle of cayenne.

Boil all this very slowly half an hour, stirring often. When done add butter the size of an egg. This dish will serve twelve people if a large tongue is used.

The mapeline and walnut ketchup may be omitted if wished though both add materially to the richness of flavor.

SARAH PRATT CARR, Seattle.

Mushroom Sauce.

Rub three tablespoons of butter with two of flour until a paste is formed. Put into a sauce pan with two good slices of onion, one bay leaf, a stalk of celery, a blade of mace and one-half dozen pepper corns; add one pint of white stock; let boil slowly for twenty minutes; strain into butter and flour which has been cooked a little; stir constantly. Add one-half can of white button mushrooms cut in half. Cook a few minutes. Stir in one cup of sweet cream, let just come to a boil.

MRS. J. C. HAINES, Seattle.

Fried Eggplant.

Slice the egg-plant and boil not longer than two minutes. Drain and dip each slice in beaten egg and then in rolled cracker crumbs. Salt and pepper and fry in plenty of hot fat to a nice brown.

ELIZABETH J. O'LEARY, Seattle.

Carrots and Green Peas.

If as sometimes happens in the best regulated households, you should not have enough green peas for the number to be served, you will find that they will combine very delightfully with young carrots.

Shell the peas and cook them alone in salted water. Scrape and cook the carrots, having sliced them very fine. Just before serving turn together, pepper, and pour over them melted butter. Serve very hot.

MISS GERTRUDE WALLACE, Stanwood.

Summer Squash.

Pare and seed a summer squash; steam or boil in a little water in the usual way; drain and mash. To a quart of squash add one-half pint of bread crumbs soaked in one-half pint of milk, one teaspoon finely minced onion, one-half teaspoon salt, one tablespoon butter, and pepper to taste, one beaten egg. Put in pudding dish and brown.

MRS. BESSIE I. SAVAGE. Seattle.

Entrees

"I go for all sharing the privileges of the government who assist in bearing its burdens—by no means excluding women."—ABRAHAM LINCOLN.

Entrees are usually made from left-overs. This is not always the case, yet more often than not these dainty dishes are a testimony of the thrift and skill of the housekeeper.

The various kinds of croquettes make up a large portion of the entrees served. From the many kinds of cold meat, they are made by simply grinding the material, and mixing with a well seasoned sauce; or they can be made richer by adding brains, mushrooms, sweetbreads, etc.

Sauce for Croquettes.

One small chopped onion cooked until tender in a tablespoon of melted butter, pour in a cup of milk and thicken with two tablespoons of flour. As you remove from the fire, add two eggs beaten, season with salt, pepper, and a little nutmeg.

Veal Croquettes.

Mix two cups of minced veal with the above sauce, shape with the fingers into balls or flat cakes. Dip in powdered bread or cracker crumbs, then in egg. Fry in smoking hot fat to a delicate brown.

Chicken Cutlets.

Mix two cups of ground chicken with one cup of cream sauce. When cold, make into pear shape, then flatten between the palms of the hands until they are one-half inch thick. Dip in egg and crumbs. Insert a piece of spaghetti an inch long in the small end to represent a bone. Fry in smoking fat, and serve with oyster sauce.

MRS. LOUISA BERRY, Lexington, Ky.

Aspic Jelly.

Aspic is made from stock, either brown or white stock highly seasoned, strained, with gelatine added. To one quart of stock add three-fourths of a box of gelatine, that has been soaked one hour in one cup cold water. Clear as for soups, allowing the white of an egg to one quart of stock. Aspic is used in many ways. As a garnish for cold meats, cold tongue and chicken are moulded in it.

Moulded in brick shaped molds, it may be sliced and served on lettuce leaves with mayonaise.

Chicken Croquettes.

Chop fine one cold boiled chicken; then take a pint of sweet milk and when the milk is boiling, stir into it two large tablespoons of flour made thin in a little cold milk; after the flour is well cooked with the milk put in a piece of butter the size of an egg. Season with salt and pepper to taste; stir all well into the chicken; roll up with your hand and dip first into an egg beaten, then into cracker rolled fine and fry in hot lard or lard and butter.

MRS. M. J. SULLIVAN, LaConner.

Scalloped Chicken.

Boil chicken until tender, cut into dice and add a small amount of the stock. Make a plain white sauce, then put into a baking pan a layer of chicken and a layer of sauce alternately then cover the top with bread crumbs. Bake until thoroughly heated through.

Make a milk gravy with the remaining stock to serve with the scalloped chicken.

Spanish Meat Balls.

One pound of round steak put through a meat grinder, one cup of moistened bread crumbs; mix well, season and make into meat balls. Partly fry one onion in butter, then one pint of tomatoes, dash of cayenne, add one cup of water. Put meat balls into this and cook slowly about two hours. It may be necessary to add more water.

Boil one cup of rice and serve with meat balls.

MRS. D. O'LEARY, Seattle.

Spaghetti, a La Italienne.

Break one-half pound of spaghetti into inch pieces, drop into a kettle of boiling water, and boil rapidly for twenty minutes; drain, pare one onion, slice, boil, add one-half can tomatoes, three tablespoons of grated cheese, salt and cayenne.

Heat all together ten minutes.

Creamed Salmon.

One can salmon minced fine, drain off liquor and throw away. Dressing: Boil one pint milk, add two tablespoons butter, salt and pepper to taste. Have ready one pint of dry bread crumbs, then place layer in bottom of buttered dish, then a layer of fish and so on having last a layer of crumbs. Pour over this the dressing and bake to a delicate brown.

HAZEL HALL, Puyallup.

Fish au Gratin.

Make a plain cream sauce, take left over fish, cut in pieces an inch or two long, arrange in a baking dish; pour over it the cream sauce, season with red pepper and salt; spread the top with buttered bread crumbs and bake.

HELEN BERRY.

Scalloped Sweetcorn.

One can of corn, one pint of milk, one cup of rolled crackers; place a layer of corn in a baking dish, season well then add layer of crackers and corn alternately. Pour the milk over it and bake.

ANNA W. SCOTT.

Cheese Custard.

Two eggs, well beaten, one cup of grated cheese, one slice of buttered bread, one cup of milk. Place the bread in bottom of baking dish and pour eggs, milk and cheese over it. Season with salt and pepper. Bake ten minutes in a quick oven and serve.

ANNA W. SCOTT, Seattle.

Salmon Pudding.

One small can of salmon, two cups of rolled crackers. Two eggs well beaten, two cups of sweet milk. Mix thoroughly and season to taste. Bake one-half hour.

ANNA W. SCOTT, Seattle.

Shrimp Pudding.

One cup shrimp, one cup grated cheese, two cups rolled crackers, good sized lump of butter. For wetting use milk or cream. Season with salt and pepper. Mix all together and bake in the oven.

W. H. SCOTT, Seattle.

Asparagus: Entree.

Put your asparagus in a baking dish, cover with cream, season with pepper and salt, cover an inch deep with grated cheese.

Timbales Regence: Mushroom Sauce.

Take one pint of cooked and blanched sweetbreads, with skin and fat removed, chop fine. Put one tablespoon of butter in frying pan, when melted add two tablespoons fine dry bread crumbs and one-half teacup of white stock; stir until the mixture boils, take from fire and stir in the sweetbreads, salt, white pepper, a dash of paprika and a little nutmeg.

Beat two eggs light and beat thoroughly into mixture. Butter timbale moulds, dust well with browned bread crumbs, fill them two-thirds full, place in baking pan half filled with boiling water and bake for twenty minutes in good oven. When done turn carefully on heated plates and serve with the following sauce about them and a garnish of water cress.

Mushroom Sauce.

Rub three tablespoons of butter with two of flour until a paste is formed. Put into a sauce pan with two good slices of onion, one bay leaf, a stalk of celery, a blade of mace and one-half dozen pepper corns; add one pint of white stock; let boil slowly for twenty minutes, strain into butter and flour, which has been cooked a little; stir constantly. Add one-half can of white button mushrooms cut in half. Cook a few minutes. Stir in one cup of sweet cream; let come to a boil and serve around timbales.

MRS. J. C. HAINES, Seattle.

Fried Bananas.

Pare six bananas, slice lengthwise in thick slices, put two tablespoons of butter in frying pan, then put in just enough fruit to cover the bottom of the pan, brown and turn and brown on the other side. Care must be taken that the slices be not broken. When served the bananas may be plain or orange juice may be squeezed over them.

MRS. D. O'LEARY, Seattle.

Fried Apples.

Slice large firm apples, have ready a frying pan containing a small amount of hot butter, just cover the bottom of the pan with the sliced apples, turn carefully after browning. Care must be taken that the slices be not broken or the attractiveness of the dish will be marred. Sprinkle with sugar and serve at once.

Spanish Rice.

Boil one teacup of rice; add one can tomatoes, six little Chili peppers, one onion. Fry the onion a little in bacon. Heat altogether; delicious.

Cook the rice Japanese style, which is: Wash well, put in tightly covered kettle with salt, butter and just covered with water. Boil hard fifteen minutes without uncovering. If it boils over move back but do not uncover. Can be made with left-over rice and tomatoes.

MRS. F. W. COTTERILL, Seattle.

Salads

"One principal cause of the failure of so many magnificent schemes, social, political, religious, which have followed each other age after age, has been this: That in almost every case they have ignored the rights and powers of one half the human race, viz., women. I believe that politics will not go right, that society will not go right, that nothing human will ever go right, except in so far as woman goes right; and to make woman go right she must be put in her place and she must have her rights."—CHARLES KINGSLEY.

Never-Fail Mayonaise Dressing.

Yolk of one egg, one tablespoon vinegar, one and one-half tablespoons water, one-fourth teaspoon salt, pinch of mustard and a little paprika. Mix well, then add olive oil and beat with a Dover egg-beater; it is not necessary to add the olive oil slowly. Five minutes' hard beating should produce perfect mayonaise.

Use the best oil and vinegar and success is sure. This dressing will keep for several days.

MISS JOSEPHINE ANDERSON, Seattle.

Cooked Salad Dressing.

Two tablespoons sugar, three eggs, one-half cup hot vinegar, one teaspoon butter, one-half teaspoon salt, one-third teaspoon mustard, mixed smooth in a little cold water, dash of cayenne pepper. Let come to a boil, remove from the stove, then add one-half cup sweet cream and beat well.

AUGUSTA ANDERSON, Seattle.

Steamed Mayonaise.

Put in a double boiler two tablespoons each of butter and olive oil, three-fourths cup cream (sweet preferred), yolks four eggs, three tablespoons of vinegar or juice of two lemons, one teaspoon sugar, salt and cayenne pepper to taste. Stir constantly.

MRS. F. W. COTTERILL, Seattle.

Salad Dressing.

Two eggs well beaten, one-half cup vinegar, teaspoon salt, one-half teaspoon mustard, one-half teaspoon white pepper, dash of cayenne. Boil together, stirring well until creamy. Remove from fire and add butter size of walnut. When cold add two tablespoons of sweet cream if desired.

Salad Dressing That Will Keep Six Months.

One and one-fourth cups vinegar, butter size of an egg, one tablespoon salt, one-fourth teaspoon cayenne, one rounded tablespoon of cornstarch, dissolved in part of the vinegar while cold, yolks three eggs well beaten, add to the cornstarch. Bring the other ingredients to a boil and stir this in. Add juice of one lemon when cold.

This mixed with half cream makes a fine cream dressing.

MRS. J. J. BOGARDUS, Seattle.

Sour Cream Dressing.

Beat light two eggs, one cup sour cream, two teaspoons sugar, then add three tablespoons vinegar. Cook in a double boiler until the mixture thickens.

Potato Salad Dressing.

One-half pint vinegar, butter the size of an egg, one egg well beaten. One teaspoon of flour mixed smoothly with one-half cup of cream or milk, one teaspoon of mustard, one of salt, one of pepper and a tablespoon of sugar. Put vinegar and butter to heat; mix other ingredients thoroughly and stir in. Cook a few minutes.

Pour over the salad while hot.

MRS. ANNA COMBES, Elma.

Chicken and Nut Salad.

Cut the white meat of a chicken into small pieces and add to a half cup of English walnuts chopped rather coarsely, a cup of finely cut celery, or four or five lettuce leaves torn into shreds. If the latter, dust lightly with celery salt and pepper.

Serve with mayonaise or other dressing if preferred.

SUSAN CURRIER ORNES.

Chicken Salad.

One chicken stewed until tender. Remove skin, bones and gristle. Cut into small pieces. Add two good-sized stalks celery cut fine. Put in a handful of water cress or crisp, tender lettuce—cress preferable. Add dressing just before serving.

This salad may be varied by putting equal parts of celery and cabbage, or take two-thirds solid white cabbage and one-third celery and add water cress.

Lobster Salad.

Use equal parts lobster and celery cut fine. Chill and squeeze the juice of a lemon over the mixture; then pour over the following dressing, being sure that the dressing is very cold.

Dressing: Stir the yolks of two eggs in a deep dish until light, add teaspoon of salt, one of sugar, one of English mustard, a little red pepper and one tablespoon of olive oil.

Melted butter may be used instead of oil. Stir until thick and light. Do not pour over the lobster until ready to serve.

MRS. ANNA M. COMBES, Elma.

Potato Salad.

Two quarts of mashed potatoes, a few onions chopped fine, two slices fried bacon chopped, a few sour pickles cut in small pieces, whites of three hard-boiled eggs also chopped.

For dressing: The fat from the fried bacon, three-fourths cup vinegar poured into the hot fat, one tablespoon sugar, one teaspoon of mustard, pinch of salt, yolks of three boiled eggs mashed fine; stir all together and cook a little. Then mix into the salad.

LINA FAIRLEY, Avon.

Potato Salad, No. 2.

Peal and boil several large potatoes, slice into a large dish, chop fine and mix in two onions, salt to taste. Mix in the potato this dressing: Scant cup vinegar, one beaten egg, one tablespoon flour rubbed with the same amount of butter, one teaspoon mustard, pinch of salt; boil a minute or two.

GRACE FORREST, Avon.

Fruit Salad.

One box gelatine dissolved in one pint of cold water. When dissolved add four pints hot water, juice of two lemons, two pints sugar; when it begins to jell add one can shredded pineapple, two oranges cut in small pieces, or any kind of fruit preferred.

MRS. B. R. McCLELLAND, Olympia.

Emergency Salad.

Use chopped apples and onions, one-tenth onions and nine-tenths apples. Serve with any salad dressing.

CLARA K. BOWERS, Seattle.

Tomato Jelly Salad.

One can tomatoes, one-half box gelatine, pepper and salt. Boil tomatoes, season high with pepper and salt, strain, add gelatine (dissolved) and fill mould. When cold cut in slices or cubes and serve on lettuce leaves with mayonnaise.

Grape Salad.

Peel and seed large white grapes, add one-fourth as much chopped celery as you have grapes and about same of walnuts.

Serve on lettuce leaves with any good dressing.

Cherry Salad.

Remove the seeds from large ripe cherries, place piece of walnut in each one. Heap fruit on lettuce leaf and serve with any good dressing.

Stuffed Tomato Salad.

Take smooth tomatoes, remove skin and scrape out inside; fill with chopped celery and just before serving place spoonful of mayonnaise on each; to which one spoonful of chopped peanuts has been added.

MRS. G. F. ZIMMERMAN, Seattle.

Cabbage Salad (Quickly Made).

Chop the cabbage fine. Sprinkle with salt, pepper and a few spoonfuls of sugar; mix well. Pour on vinegar to taste, and stir well; lastly a cup of thick cream; mix again and it is ready to serve. Some like onion chopped with the cabbage.

MRS. RENA FORREST, Anacortes.

Apple Salad.

Eight apples and one bunch of celery chopped fine, one cup of nuts.

Dressing: Two eggs, scant half cup sugar, one tablespoon melted butter, teaspoon mustard, half teaspoon salt; beat well together, then add one-half cup of vinegar. Put all together cold, then cook until thick. When cold pour over the salad.

MRS. F. L. BAILEY, LaConner.

Bean-Potato Salad.

One pint of cold boiled potatoes diced, one-half pint wax beans cut slant wise, one heaping tablespoon of minced young onion and one of parsley. Serve with any good salad dressing.

MRS. D. O'LEARY, Seattle.

Hot Slaw.

One teaspoon mustard, two eggs, one cup vinegar, one tablespoon sugar, one tablespoon butter, one cup cream. Heat this all together and stir into it your cabbage chopped fine. This is enough dressing to fix slaw for a dozen persons; so use half the recipe for the usual family.

MISS MARTHA JENNINGS. LaConner.

Novel Beet Salad.

Boil the same number of large beets as you have persons to serve. When done remove skin and scoop out carefully a hole at one end about the size of a plum. Set the beets in a jar of vinegar for several hours. Chop the scoopings of the beets and mix with salt, pepper, and half as much chopped onion as you have chopped beets; add chopped celery or celery salt, and chopped green peppers. Mix all together with a mayonnaise dressing to the consistency of a hash. Then pack into the hollow beets, spread over again with the dressing and place an olive or a slice of boiled egg thereon. Serve on a small plate garnished with a lettuce leaf.

MRS. NELLIE MITCHELL FICK, Seattle.

Washington or A. Y. P. Fruit Salad.

Chop one Yakima apple, one banana, one dozen English walnuts, three long sticks of celery and mix together with a mayonnaise salad dressing. Place on three plates, each garnished with a lettuce leaf, spread over with whipped cream and arrange half slices of one orange around the edges, and three Kennewick strawberries on top the cream. Serve cold.

MRS. NELLIE MITCHELL FICK.

Fruit Salad.

Three oranges, one-half dozen bananas, one-half cup English walnuts, one-half cup seeded raisins, one small cup sugar over fruit (candied cherries help) also one-half cup canned pineapple.

Take one-fourth package gelatine dissolved in a little cold water; pour over this two cups boiling water; strain and when cold pour over the fruit. Let stand until the gelatine sets.

MRS. CHAS. HARRIS, Bellingham.

Grape Fruit Salad.

Cut in two, remove seeds and membranes, fill cavity with white grapes, with ice around. This makes a very pretty dish.

Luncheon Salad.

Pour boiling water over nice, large, ripe tomatoes, the skins may be easily removed. Place on ice until quite cold, then serve one large tomato on lettuce leaf; cut a square from the top and fill with a mixture of chopped green onions and cucumbers. Put mayonnaise on top. This makes a very pretty dish.

MRS. ROBERT BERRY, Bellingham.

Waldorf Salad.

Cut crisp lettuce leaves into strips with scissors, pare one large orange, cut into cubes, chop a few nuts and sprinkle over; use any salad dressing preferred, toss with a fork and arrange on lettuce leaves.

Peach Salad.

Take one dozen tart peaches, one and one-half cups of finely cut hearts of celery, one cup of finely chopped nuts. Use any salad dressing preferred.

Carrot Salad.

One quart of sliced carrots boiled tender. Three large long, red peppers, mashed to a pulp, also mash a clove of garlic; equal parts of olive oil and vinegar as a dressing. Mix peppers, garlic and dressing thoroughly, and pour over the carrots. Let stand about two hours.

MRS. D. O'LEARY, Seattle.

My Potato Salad.

Cold boiled potatoes cut into dice (never chop), add onion, salt and pepper, to taste. Pour over the boiled salad dressing and mix well. This is better after a few hours on ice.

Mayonnaise Dressing with Pure Olive Oil.

Break into deep bowl one egg, beat one-half minute with Dover egg beater, add one-third cup oil, one-half teaspoon at a time not stopping the beating. When thick add juice of one-half lemon.

This is a very quick way to make dressing for vegetable salads, though not quite so thick as desired for fruit salads.

MRS. MILDRED KYLE.

Salads and Salad Dressing.

The most delicious salads can be made by combining vegetables, such as peas, string beans and cauliflower, or any vegetable you may have cooked. I like my cooked dressing better than mayonnaise for potato salad.

Fruits can also be combined with great success. Apples and celery together, or apples and nuts, cannot be excelled. Tomatoes stuffed with nuts and celery are fine.

Boiled Salad Dressing.

One small cup cider vinegar, one tablespoon sugar, lump of butter, one-half teaspoon mixed mustard, heat to near boiling point, pour slowly into well beaten yolks of two eggs. Set the bowl into boiling water on the stove and stir until thick. When cold this can be thinned to proper consistency with cream for potato or any vegetable salad.

Fruit Salad.

Two cups apple, two cups orange, two cups banana, two cups pineapple, cut in small blocks. Pour Golden Dressing over fruit and let stand about two hours before serving. The canned sliced pineapple is preferable.

VIRGINIA M. ELDER.

Vegetables

"What is politics? Why, it's housekeeping on a big scale. The government is in a muddle, because it has been trying to do the housekeeping without the women."

Because of our vegetation department we have not presented many recipes in this, simply because we did not care to repeat and because the vegetarian department covers the ground so well.

Burgess Potatoes.

Take cold boiled potatoes firm of texture, chop fine. For a quart of chopped potatoes place one tablespoon butter and one of lard in a frying pan. When hot add the potatoes salted and peppered and heat very thoroughly, but do not brown; serve hot.

CLARA KURTZ BOWERS, Seattle.

Stuffed Potatoes.

Select potatoes of a uniform size, wash and bake. When baked, cut off one end, using a sharp knife that the edges may be clean cut and not ragged. Scrape out the contents of the potatoes carefully, preserving the shells; mash the potato well and season with pepper and salt, then stir into it two beaten eggs and half a cup of sweet cream; fill the shells and place the caps in position. Return to the oven and heat well; serve very hot.

MRS. S. L. W. CLARK.

Hashed Brown Potatoes.

Chop the potatoes with a slaw chopper, season with a little onion, pepper and salt. Melt a tablespoon of butter in a skillet or use drippings from bacon. When hot, put in the potatoes and press down close to the skillet. It will brown in a little while. Turn as an omelet and serve very hot.

MRS. LOUISA BERRY, Lexington, Ky.

Potato Omelet.

Add an egg to left over potatoes and brown in salt pork

fat; then season with pepper and salt to taste. Turn into the serving dish in the form of an omelet and garnish with parsley.

MRS. ESTERBROOK, Bellingham.

Rice Tomatoes.

Cook one can tomatoes twenty minutes with salt, pepper and lump of butter. Add one cup of cream with one tablespoon of flour well mixed; stir until smooth. Then add one cup of well cooked rice. This will serve ten persons.

MRS. G. F. ZIMMERMAN, Seattle.

Stuffed Tomatoes (Cooked).

Take six firm ripe tomatoes; cut a thin slice from the top; hollow a little and season the tomato slightly. Then one cup of cold meat that has been put through the food chopper, one-half cup of powdered bread crumbs moistened with one egg; season with onion juice and salt. Make into balls and place in the hollow of the tomato. Put them in a pan containing one-half cup water and two tablespoons of butter. Bake an hour in a moderate oven.

MRS. D. O'LEARY, Seattle.

Egyptian Rice.

A delectable dish to be served with baked fish. One small onion fried in butter but not browned, to which add one can of tomatoes and one-half cup rice, which has been previously well cooked, also salt and pepper. Bake twenty minutes.

MRS. ANNA B. MEYER, Seattle.

Stuffed Peppers.

Soak one-half dozen green peppers in salt water over night, clear of seeds and stuff with one cup of chopped veal, one large tomato chopped, one-half cup bread crumbs, butter, pepper and salt.

Bake in a little soup stock for one-half hour.

MRS. ANNA B. MEYER, Seattle.

Baked Beans.

Two quarts beans, one-half cup syrup, one-fourth cup brown sugar, two or three slices of bacon, salt, pepper and mustard to taste. Parboil beans, then put in a bean jar or a pan and add other ingredients; cover with boiling water and bake at lest four hours; longer is better.

MARY E. WALTERMIRE.

Baked Beans.

One quart beans, parboil in clear water, drain, place in bake pan, add two tablespoons molasses, one pound pork, one-half teaspoon mustard, teaspoon sugar, salt to taste. Bake in oven all day. Keep covered with water and a tight lid. This dish is all the better for being warmed over.

HARRY E. MITTLESTAD, Avon.

To Can Green Vegetables.

Pack the green vegetables (beans, corn, etc.) in Mason jars; fill full of cold water, secure tops on tight; turn upside down to see if tight. Place in boiler having first placed a shingle or board on bottom of the boiler. Fill with water half way up the jars and boil one hour, covered so they will steam. MRS. KATE PLUM, Bellingham.

Keeping Boiled Corn Hot.

To keep corn hot for out of doors dinners or picnics, boil with the husks on and it will keep hot for hours and be most sweet and delicious.

MRS. ALMA A. WILLIAMS, Mt. Vernon.

Scalloped Sweetcorn.

One can of corn, one pint of milk, one cup of rolled crackers. Place a layer of corn in baking dish, season well, then add layer of crackers and corn alternately. Pour the milk over it and bake. ANNA W. SCOTT, Seattle.

Corn Fritters.

To the contents of one can of corn add two eggs, beat well, add salt and pepper, one cup of sweet milk, two teaspoons baking powder and flour to make a stiff batter. Drop from a spoon into hot lard and fry to nice brown.

MRS. E. P. FRENCH.

Beets.

Beets are usually served as a pickle with vinegar dressing, but simply as a vegetable this way will be found very pleasing.

Boil the beets as usual taking great care that the skin is not broken so that they will bleed, and lose their color.

When done remove the skin and slice, season well with salt and pepper, and pour over them melted butter; stir well so that every slice will get some of the butter. Serve very hot.

MRS. FLORA A. P. ENGLE, Coupeville.

Stewed Cabbage.

Slice the cabbage fine and evenly; sprinkle with salt and put into stew kettle; cover with boiling water and cook about half an hour or until tender. Cook without cover to the kettle. When done drain in a collander, pepper well and dot with bits of butter.

MRS. ZOE KEITH JONES, Seattle.

A Simple Way to Cook Carrots.

The carrots should be young and tender, old carrots are never good. Scrape and cut in small pieces. Cook in salted water until tender; drain and sprinkle well with pepper and pour over them a small quantity of melted butter.

Creamed Celery.

Cut celery into inch pieces and cook in salted water until tender. Drain and pour over two cups of sweet milk; return to the stove and thicken slightly; add pepper and a dash of cayenne.

Green Corn Fritters.

One pint of grated green corn, three eggs, two tablespoons of milk, one tablespoon of melted butter, one teaspoon of salt, beat the eggs well, add the corn by degrees, also the milk and butter, thicken with just enough flour to hold together. One teaspoon of baking powder should be put in the flour.

Have ready a kettle of hot fat; drop the corn from a spoon into the fat and fry brown.

MRS. BERT ESTERBROOK, Bellingham.

Cheese Dishes

Welsh Rarebit.

One cup hot sweet milk, one-fourth pound grated cheese, one-half teaspoon of salt, one-fourth teaspoon mustard, dash of cayenne, one teaspoon flour, one egg well beaten, one teaspoon butter.

Mix cheese, flour, egg, mustard, salt and pepper. Add heated milk a little at a time to cheese mixture until as smooth as cream. Pour over toasted crackers or bread.

Never Fail Welsh Rarebit (For Twelve Persons).

One pound of American cheese, one pint of milk, two eggs, two tablespoons each of flour and butter creamed together, one-half teaspoon of mustard, one-half teaspoon of salt and one-half teaspoon of paprika.

Light the lamp, discard the outer pan and put in the inner pan one pint of milk, allow it to come to the boiling point and add the creamed paste of flour and butter; stir this slowly until dissolved, then put in the cheese, cut into small pieces. When this is melted, before shutting off the lamp, stir in the well beaten eggs and allow it to cook for one minute. Serve this on hot toast or crackers.

MRS. NELLIE MITCHELL FICK, Seattle.

Cheese Straws.

W. S. C. Domestic Science Dept.

One cup grated cheese, almost one cup flour, one cup fresh bread crumbs, one tablespoon butter, one speck each of white and red pepper. Four tablespoons milk or water, cream butter, add flour, crumbs and cheese, then add seasoning, mix thoroughly, add milk last, roll gently one-fourth inch thick, cut in strips one-fourth inch wide, bake until brown in a moderate oven.

Small rings may be made from the same dough to hold straws.

Cheese Fondu.

Place one tablespoon of butter in the chafing dish; when melted add one cup fresh milk, one cup fine bread crumbs, two cups of grated cheese, one saltspoon of mustard, and a little cayenne. Stir constantly and add two eggs beaten light just before serving.

MISS EVELYN JOHNSON, LaConner.

Cheese Canaps.

Mix one and one-half cups grated cheese with one-half teaspoon salt and a little cayenne; add the well beaten whites of three eggs. Pile on thin slices of bread and brown in the oven.

MRS. BERT ESTERBROOK, Bellingham.

Cheese Salad.

Two cream cheese, one tablespoon melted butter, one tablespoon cream worked together. Have ready one hard boiled egg chopped, one ten cent bottle stuffed olives chopped, and a very little onion, also chopped. Put this with the cheese. Mould all together and put in a tin; spread until it is about one inch thick. Serve with salad dressing. This will serve about ten people. Cut in squares and put on lettuce leaves with one spoon of salad dressing on each.

MRS. G. HENSLER, Anacortes.

Cheese Balls.

Grate American cheese, add melted butter, cayenne, and salt to taste; roll in chopped parsley and serve on crisp crackers.

MRS. BERT ESTERBROOK, Bellingham.

Cheese Omelet.

Beat three eggs and add to them one tablespoon milk, and a tablespoon grated cheese. Cook as in the case of the usual omelet: add a little more cheese before folding; turn it out on a hot dish and grate cheese over it before serving.

HELEN J. BERRY, Bellingham.

Breakfast and Luncheon

"Ah! it is women who have given the costliest hostages to fortune. Out into the battle of life she has sent her best beloved with fearful odds against them. Oh! by the dangers she has dared; by the hours of patient watching, by bedsides where helpless children lay; by the incense of ten thousand prayers wafted to Heaven from their gentle lips. I charge you, grant them the power to protect along life's treacherous highways those they have so loved."—FRANCIS E. WILLARD.

Toast.

The plain or buttered dry toast that is so often seen on our breakfast tables may be delicious or quite the reverse according to how it is prepared.

The bread should not be too dry nor sliced thin, have a hot fire so that the toast may be browned while yet soft in the middle. It is impossible to have good toast from poor bread.

French Toast.

Beat two eggs and add one teacup of sweet milk, into this dip slices of bread and fry a nice brown.

Fried Rolls.

Mix bread sponge up stiff at night, kneading it stiff enough to make into loaves, let stand all night. In the morning cut off in slices; fry as you would doughnuts. This makes a fine hot bread for breakfast.

MRS. CHAS. HARRIS, Bellingham.

Eggs, Soft Boiled.

Put the eggs into a deep porcelain vessel, pour over them boiling water to the depth of two inches above the eggs. Cover and set on the very back of the stove or on the reservoir for ten or twelve minutes.

When broken the white will be a soft jelly. This is a most wholesome way to serve eggs, and a decided improvement on the old way of boiling three minutes.

Plain Omelet.

Six eggs, whites beaten stiff and yolks to a foam; half cup rich milk, salt and pepper, added to the yolks and all stirred lightly into the whites; have skillet hot and greased with butter; pour in mixture, set in oven until done; fold over and serve at once on hot platter.

This is a good foundation for many different kinds of omelet. Jelly, chopped ham or cold meat of any kind may be added or chopped oysters make a dainty omelet.

MRS. R. H. BALL, La Conner.

Scrambled Eggs.

Put into a skillet one cup of rich milk (cream and milk is better) break into it eight eggs; stir slightly enough to break the yolks and mix with the whites; season with pepper and salt and serve while quite soft.

This is very nice served on toast.

Stuffed Eggs.

Boil eggs ten minutes and then plunge into cold water. Shell, remove yolk from whites and place in bowl. Add tablespoon of butter for twelve eggs, salt and pepper to taste, a teaspoon each of celery seed, mustard (ground), a little chopped parsley, mix well, adding juice of lemon. Stuff whites and serve cold.

MRS. G. F. ZIMMERMAN, Seattle.

Eggs Poached in Milk.

Be sure that the eggs are absolutely fresh. Fill a pan with sweet milk and heat almost to boiling; break eggs into it, taking care that the milk does not burn. When poached remove to platter and sprinkle with salt, pepper, and bits of butter.

This is much superior to eggs poached in water.

MARTHA JENNINGS, LaConner.

Shirred Eggs.

Set in oven until hot a common white dish large enough to hold the number of eggs to be cooked; put in small piece of butter, break the eggs carefully one at a time, sprinkle with salt and pepper. The addition of a tablespoon of cream

to every two eggs is a great improvement. Allow eggs to cook three to five minutes.
MISS ROSALIE KELLOGG, LaConner.

A Breakfast Dish.

Chop some cold meat and put some milk on stove to boil, and thicken just a little, season with salt and pepper. Toast some slices of bread, then pour this mixture over the toast.

Meat broth can be used in place of milk. Excellent if nicely prepared.

Scalloped Potatoes.

Pare and slice thin, raw potatoes. Put a layer of potatoes in a granite pan, sprinkle with pepper and salt and small pieces of butter; sift a tablespoon of flour over them; add another layer of potatoes, season as before; repeat until the pan is full, having the seasoning on top. Before putting in oven pour in enough milk to come to the top of pan. Bake in a moderate oven until done.
MRS. JOHN CHILBERG, La Conner.

Potato Balls.

Boil half a dozen potatoes and grate or mash them. Put in three eggs, salt and pepper to taste; add enough flour to make into balls. Fry in hot fat as you would doughnuts.
MRS. PETER DOWNEY, La Conner.

Luncheon Relish.

Take nine good-sized potatoes, pare them and put to cook in a porcelain kettle; add to them two pounds of boneless salt fish and cook until done. Season with butter or cream to taste; beat to a cream and serve hot with toast.
MRS. ALMA A. WILLIAMS, Mt. Vernon.

Breakfast Potatoes.

Dice the potatoes into small cubes; have fat hot on stove and turn potatoes into it; stir often; when done turn cream into them; salt and pepper to taste.
MRS. C. ALVERSON, La Conner.

Creamed Codfish.

Cut a pound package of boneless codfish into small

pieces and soak in plenty of water. Pour off the water and cook in water, just letting it come to a boil (long cooking will make it tough). Pour off the water and cover with milk; heat to boiling point; remove to back of stove and stir in two beaten eggs. If you want it very nice, indeed, slice four hard-boiled eggs and stir in just as you serve.

LINDA JENNINGS.

Dutch "Pon-Hoss."

Take four pigs feet and hocks, four pounds lean fresh pork, two pounds calf's liver; boil until meat falls from bones, strain the liquor off the meat, remove all the bones, grind meat through meat grinder, put back into the liquor and season well with salt and black pepper; thicken with cornmeal to the consistency of mush; boil one hour and mold. This is delicious cold for lunch or is excellent fried.

MAY ARKWRIGHT HUTTON,
President Woman Suffrage Club, Spokane, Wash.

Sausage.

Ten pounds meat, six tablespoon salt, two tablespoons pepper, one tablespoon of sage. Cut the meat into small pieces, as I find that the grinder feeds better if the pieces are not too large. Before grinding put a layer of meat in a pan and sprinkle with salt and pepper, then another layer and so on. When it is ground the sausage will be evenly seasoned.

MRS. MATTIE M. METIER.

Sandwiches

Sandwiches require good bread, and the bread should not be too fresh, then care in the making that they be dainty in appearance. The butter should be softened to spread nicely, and all meat should be ground or sliced thin as a wafer.

Sandwiches are cut in many fancy shapes with cutters made especially for the purpose.

Nut Sandwiches.

Chop English walnuts very fine, mix with whipped cream and put between thin slices of white bread. You may use dates the same way.

Another good filling for sandwiches is cream cheese sprinkled with chopped walnuts.

Water Cress Sandwiches.

Wash and dry the cress, mix with hard-boiled eggs chopped very fine, with a slight sprinkling of lemon juice.

Cheese Sandwiches.

These are very nice. Take one hard-boiled egg, a quarter of a pound of common cheese, grated, one-half teaspoon salt, one-quarter teaspoon mustard, one tablespoon melted butter and one-quarter teaspoon of vinegar. Crumble the yolk of the egg fine in a small bowl, put in the butter and mix it smooth with a spoon, then add the salt, pepper, mustard and cheese, mixing well; lastly put in the vinegar.

Sandwich Dressing.

Yolks of three hard-boiled eggs, one teaspoon of made mustard, one-half teaspoon of pepper, one of salt, two tablespoons of vinegar, and one large tablespoon of olive oil; chop the meat fine; mix dressing with the meat and spread between thin slices of bread.

EDITH JEWETT, Avon.

Ham Sandwiches.

Chop cold boiled ham, fat and lean together; to a cup of the chopped ham allow one teaspoon of melted butter, the yolks of two hard-boiled eggs, add lemon juice, salt and pepper to taste; spread on thin slices of bread.

HELEN J. BERRY, Bellingham.

Club Sandwiches.

They are made of thin slices of buttered toast, cut off edges; on this place a leaf of crisp lettuce, a very thin slice of roast chicken, slice of bacon or ham, and thin slices of ripe tomatoes. May be served with meat and toast hot.

HELEN J. BERRY, Bellingham.

Lettuce Sandwiches.

Place crisp leaves of lettuce with salad dressing between thin slices of buttered bread.

Cheese Sandwiches.

One package of Neuchatel cheese, mix in a bowl with enough tomato catsup to make a paste; spread between buttered Long Branch crackers.

R. H. BERRY.

Bread

"Taxation without representation is tyranny."

Bread has truly been called "the staff of life," and the ability to make a good loaf of bread will add much to the material comfort of a home. It is impossible to make good bread with poor flour, so to buy cheap flour is not economy, but quite the reverse.

Bread.

Scald one quart of milk, cook four medium-sized potatoes; when lukewarm mash with both one cup yeast, stir together with enough flour to make batter; knead in morning about twenty minutes; raise again light, shape into loaves and raise again.

MRS. G. W. JOHNSON, La Conner.

Yeast.

Boil pinch of hops in about a quart of water. Take four raw potatoes, grate and stir into the water; put in half teacup suger, one-fourth teacup salt, teaspoon ginger, one tablespoon flour; use one yeast cake to start. This yeast will keep for some time.

MRS. G. W. JOHNSON, La Conner.

Yeast No. 2.

Soak a yeast cake in a half cup warm water. Then take three cups of mashed potatoes, four tablespoons flour, tablespoon of salt and two tablespoons of sugar; scald with about two teacups of hot water, or enough water to make the yeast like porridge; when just warm add the soaked yeast cake. Keep in a warm place until fermentation is completed.

MRS. ISAAC JENNINGS, La Conner.

Bread.

Take two quarts of warm water and yeast No. 2, stir in enough flour to make stiff batter; do this at night. In the morning knead thoroughly, let raise again; when light shape into loaves, and raise again. It is well to warm and grease the bread pans, as putting the bread into cold pans will chill it.

MRS. ISAAC JENNINGS, La Conner.

Unleavened Parker House Rolls.

One quart flour, rub into it three tablespoons cold butter, having first sifted the flour with three teaspoons of baking powder; beat one egg and add to it enough milk to make a pint of wetting; roll quite thin and dip each biscuit into melted butter. Put in the pan, folding them half over.

MRS. WM. WALDRIP, Coupeville.

Cream Biscuit.

One quart flour, sifted with three teaspoons baking powder, rub into this three tablespoons thick sour cream; use sweet milk to make a soft dough; roll out about a third of an inch thick; cut out the biscuits and bake in a quick oven. LINDA JENNINGS.

Sally Lunns.

Two cups buttermilk, dissolve in it one teaspoon soda, add one beaten egg, and two tablespoons melted butter; use enough flour to make a nice batter; make in gem pans in very hot oven. MADGE JENNINGS.

Tea Biscuits.

One quart flour, one-half cup butter and lard mixed, two teaspoons baking powder, one teaspoon salt and two of sugar. Use enough sweet milk to make the usual biscuit dough; then knead just as you do yeast bread and set away for four or five hours in a cool place. Roll out and bake.

MRS. W. L. THOMPSON, Seattle.
(From Good Housekeeping.)

Graham Gems.

One cup graham flour, one-half cup white flour, sugar and salt, one egg, one cup milk. Baking powder one large teaspoon. Beat and let stand about ten minutes.

Brown Bread.

Two cups sour milk, one-half cup molasses, one-half cup raisins, one cup flour, two cups meal, a little salt, one teaspoon baking powder, two teaspoons soda. Steam two and one-half hours.

     MRS. NANCY CURTIS, Houghton.

Graham Bread with Raisins.

One pint sour milk, small teaspoon of soda, half graham flour and half white to make stiff batter, three tablespoons molasses, one-half cup sugar, raisins one cup.

     MRS. CARRIE OAKLEY, Anacortes.

Graham Drop Cakes.

One egg, one cup sugar, two tablespoons lard, two tablespoons molasses, one cup sour milk, one-half cup chopped raisins, salt, cinnamon and nutmeg, one teaspoon soda. Graham flour to stiffen and drop on greased pan by teaspoons full. MRS. CLARA SAUERS, Aberdeen.

Graham Muffins.

One egg, two tablespoons butter, one tablespoon sugar, beaten together, one-half cup sweet milk, now add one cup graham or whole-wheat flour, in which was previously stirred one teaspoon of baking powder. Bake in rings twenty minutes in a hot oven.

     MRS. A. L. CALLOW, Elma.

Waffles.

Three eggs; put yolks in big bowl and whites in small; one pint milk, well stirred with yolks, level teaspoon salt, rounding teaspoon sugar; sift in three cups flour with two heaping teaspoons baking powder, beat hard, then add three tablespoons melted butter, lastly the whites beaten stiff. Have waffle iron hot and do not use too much grease.

     MISS E. M. HIBBS, San Diego, Cal.

Waffles No. 2.

Two eggs well beaten, two tablespoons of melted butter (cream is good if you have it), one pint milk, one teaspoon of baking powder, stir in enough flour to make thin batter. Have waffle irons very hot. This recipe also makes very good pop-overs.   HELEN J. BERRY.

Waffles No. 3.

One egg, two cups sour milk or butter milk, one tablespoon melted butter, one teaspoon soda and enough flour to make thin batter. Made by this recipe waffles will not fall.

MARTHA JENNINGS.

Potato Pancakes.

Peal and grate five large potatoes, drain off the juice, add two well-beaten eggs to the potato, salt to taste, beat well and fry like pancakes with plenty of fat.

NETTIE SCHERBERT, Avon.

Pancakes.

Two cups butter-milk, one egg, one teaspoon salt, one teaspoon sugar, one teaspoon soda dissolved in a small portion of the buttermilk, flour to make nice batter.

MISS ELLEN GRAHAM, Avon.

Lemon Crackers.

Two and one-half cups sugar, one cup lard, two eggs, one pint sweet milk, five cents' worth bakers' ammonia, five cents' worth lemon oil, a little salt and flour enough to roll out thin like crackers.

MRS. SUSAN GRIFFITH, Bellingham.

Sally Lunns.

Beat three eggs, two pints of flour rubbed with butter size of an egg, two teaspoons baking powder. Mix with sweet milk to a nice batter. Bake in gem pans. Nice for tea. MRS. LOUSIA BERRY, Lexington, Ky.

Biscuit.

Pint of flour, heaping teaspoon baking powder, work in tablespoon of cotosuet or butter. Mix with sweet milk as soft as can be handled. Roll out and bake in very hot oven.

This is an excellent recipe for shortcake if you double the amount of shortening.

MRS. HELEN J. BERRY, Bellingham.

Sour Milk Biscuit.

Ont cup milk (sour), one-third teaspoon soda, two tablespoons melted lard, one teaspoon baking powder in the flour.

Mix with a spoon and roll out. This makes them much lighter than with soda alone and will not be yellow.

MRS. CHAS. HARRIS, Bellingham.

Beaten Biscuit.

Mix one quart of flour with one iron spoon or two tablespoons of lard and one full teaspoon of salt. Make into a stiff dough with ice water. Work on a kneader or beat with a mallet until smooth and glossy. Roll, cut into shape, pierce with a fork and bake about twenty or twenty-five minutes.

MRS. LOUISA BERRY, Lexington, Ky.

Parker House Rolls.

Rub one-half tablespoon of butter and a half tablespoon of lard into two quarts of sifted flour; into a well in the middle pour one pint of cold boiled milk, add half a cup of yeast, half a cup of sugar and a little salt; mix well.

If wanted for night prepare this the night before; in the morning stir up, knead and let rise slowly; when light roll out with round cake cutter, put a little melted butter on one-half and lap the other half nearly over. Place in a pan about three-quarters of an inch apart. Let rise again and bake quickly.

Corn or "Johnnie" Cake.

One egg, one teacup or half pint of flour. Two teacups of cornmeal, two teacups sour milk or buttermilk, a teaspoon of soda, four heaping teaspoons of sugar and a trifle of salt if wanted.

This cake can be made for a small family with half the quantity of each article.

HARRIET E. DeVOE, Seattle.

Steamed Brown Bread.

One cup of sweet milk, two cups of sour milk, three cups of cornmeal and two cups flour, or graham, one cup molasses, one teaspoon soda; steam three hours.

MRS. JENNIE DAVIDSON.

Brown Bread.

One cup cornmeal, two cups graham flour, one cup molasses, two cups sour milk, one teaspoon soda. Boil or steam two and a half hours, then place in the oven for a few minutes to brown.

A few raisins added will improve this bread.

Pop-Overs.

Two cups milk, two cups flour, three eggs, salt. Sift flour and put in eggs and salt, then add milk a little at a time. Beat very hard (the batter will be very thin); bake in quite hot oven about twenty minutes. Should be very light when done.

Are nice split and filled with whipped cream sweetened and flavored. Do not put in baking powder.

MRS. F. W. COTTRILL, Seattle.

Quick Nut Bread.

Sift together four cups of white flour, one cup of white sugar, four rounded teaspoons of baking powder, one teaspoon of salt; add one cup of chopped nuts—walnuts or hickory—one cup of sweet milk, two well-beaten eggs. Mix well; butter two bread tins, put in the mixture, let it stand twenty minutes, then bake from thirty to forty minutes.

MRS. O. W. HARDEN, San Diego.

Nut Rolls.

When bread is ready for pans, pinch off enough for as many rolls as wished—the rolls are better if not too large—and knead in well the following: For one dozen rolls cream together butter size of walnut and two heaping tablespoons sugar. Then add two-thirds large coffee cup walnuts chopped quite fine. Add flour while kneading until quite stiff. Let rise a long time and bake in moderate oven about forty minutes. MISS MARY TOMLIN, Kirkland.

Bread.

The favorite bread for the vegetarian is unfermented whole-wheat or graham flour bread, but both can be made into delicious raised bread if preferred. I will give my recipe for graham bread, used for twenty-five years, that cannot be excelled.

Scald one cup of coarse graham flour with one cup of boiling water, add one cup of cold water and one cup of dry graham, two tablespoons of sugar; mix all with two cups of light white bread sponge. If too soft, mix into loaves with white flour and put into bread tins and raise slowly. Bake in moderate oven.

Whole-Wheat Bread.

Four cups of light white bread sponge; stir into this whole-wheat flour until as stiff as can be mixed with an iron spoon. Put into bread tins and raise until very light; bake in moderate oven.

"Mrs. Wardall's Prison Fare."

(Best ever eaten.)

Heat a large sheet-iron bread pan on the top of stove, oil very slightly with butter or Ko-nut. Mix two cups of coarse graham flour with two cups of cold water. Stir quickly and drop in spoonsful in the hot pan and bake in very hot oven until brown and crisp. Must be made fresh every morning for the day.

Rice Corn Bread.

Two cups of cornmeal, one cup cooked rice, pour over this one cup boiling water; then thin with cold water to smooth batter, season with salt and pour into bread pan and bake rather slowly until crisp. Very nutritious.

MRS. MILDRED KYLE.

Tender Graham Gems.

Two cups sweet milk, teaspoon baking powder, two tablespoons sugar, one-half teaspoon salt, tablespoon melted butter or oil; stir in enough graham flour for a moderately thick batter, drop into hot gem tins and bake in hot oven.

ANNA WARDALL SCOTT.

Desserts

"Women do not ask for the ballot as a right or a privilege, but the social and political conditions of to-day make it necessary that women be given the ballot to do their work in the world as they always have done."—
MISS JANE ADDAMS.

PUDDING SAUCES.

Lemon Sauce.

Two cups hot water, one cup sugar, three large tablespoons cornstarch, one tablespoon butter, juice and grated rind of one lemon. Boil water and sugar together five minutes, add cornstarch wet in cold water, cook in double boiler ten minutes, add butter and lemon juice last.

HARRIET E. WRIGHT, South Bellingham.

Milk Sauce.

Two-thirds cup milk, one-half cup sugar, quarter cup butter. Put all together and let come to a boil, then take off the fire and beat slowly into it one well-beaten egg.

MRS. ANNA B. HYDE, Columbia City.

Egg Sauce.

melted, stir in two well-beaten eggs and flavor.
One cup sugar, one cup boiling water or milk. When

Strawberry Sauce.

One-half cup butter creamed with one cup white sugar, stir into this one large cup of strawberries washed and mashed smooth.

Hard Sauce.

One cup of powdered sugar, one-quarter cup butter, whites of two eggs, one teaspoon vanilla. Beat the butter very hard and add the sugar, gradually beating until very light. Add the whites of the eggs one at a time and lastly the flavoring. Beat very light.

MISS ROSALIE KELLOGG, Portland.

English Plum Pudding.

One and one-half pounds of Muscatel raisins, one and three-quarters pounds of currants, one pound of Sultana raisins, two pounds of moist sugar, two pounds of bread crumbs (or flour), sixteen eggs, two pounds finely chopped suet, six ounces mixed candied peel, one ounce grated nutmeg, one ounce ground cinnamon, one-half ounce of pounded bitter almonds, the rind of two lemons grated, one-half pint milk.

Stone the raisins, wash and dry the currants, slice the candied peel, grate the bread crumbs, mix all the dry ingredients, then add the eggs well beaten. Stir in the milk and when all is thoroughly mixed put it in well-buttered moulds or pudding cloths; tie down tight and boil six or eight hours. Have the water boiling when the pudding is put in and keep it boiling.

MRS. R. RAWLINS, La Conner.

Plum Pudding.

Three-fourths of a bowl of suet—bowl to hold one and one-half pints—two teaspoons salt, one bowl sweet milk, six eggs, one bowl brown sugar, one-fourth pound citron, two bowls raisins, five or six cups flour—enough to make stiff batter—four teaspoons baking powder, flavor with one grated nutmeg. Boil three and one-half hours. Put fruit in last after being floured. Scald pudding bag and sift over with flour. An old English recipe.

MRS. CARRIE OAKLEY, Anacortes.

Steamed Pudding.

One cup molasses, one cup butter, one cup brown sugar, one cup sour milk, one cup raisins, two cups flour, two eggs, one teaspoon soda, spices to taste; steam three hours.

Sauce—One-half cup butter and one cup sugar mixed to a cream, one and one-half cups boiling water, thickened to the consistency of thick cream, flavor to taste; pour while hot over butter and sugar and whip until light and foamy.

MRS. L. A. BLAIR, Elma.

Banana Cream.

Four cups milk, one-half cup sugar, tablespoon of gelatine dissolved in warm water or milk, two eggs, well beaten.

Slice two bananas, place in dish, heat milk, stir in beaten eggs, add sugar and gelatine and pour over bananas. Serve with cream or milk.

MRS. CARRIE N. OAKLEY, Anacortes.

Orange Marmalade Pudding.

Two cups bread crumbs, one cup chopped suet, one egg, one thirty-cent jar Dundee marmalade, one teaspoon soda, scant one-half cup sweet milk. Put in moulds and steam three hours.

Sauce for same—One-half cup butter, yolks two eggs. Put in double boiler and stir until it thickens. Beat whites of two eggs and stir in just before serving; nutmeg if desired.

MRS. G. HENSLER, Anacortes.

Puff Pudding.

One pint of milk, five eggs, seven tablespoons flour, pinch of salt. Bake slowly in gem tins and eat hot with hard sauce. Delicious.

MRS. LYDIA D. ALLOMD, Anacortes.

Browned Rice and Raisins.

Brown rice in the oven to a golden brown. Take half a cup rice and half cup raisins and cook from one to two hours. Serve when cool or nearly so with nut cream, made from almond butter or with dairy cream.

MISS GERTRUDE WALLACE, Stanwood.

Mysterious Pudding.

Two eggs, their weight in flour, butter and sugar, one teaspoon baking powder, mixed with flour and sugar. Cream the butter, then add sugar and flour, four tablespoons of marmalade. Beat the yolks and whites separately, adding whites last; when well mixed pour into buttered mould and steam one and one-half hours. Serve with sweet sauce.

MISS E. M. HIBBS, San Diego, Cal.

Rice Pudding.

Three quarts milk, one-half cup uncooked rice, sweeten to taste, one-fourth teaspoon nutmeg. Bake slowly four hours. If properly cooked, when done the rice will be whole and the milk like good cream. An old New Jersey recipe and the secret is in the slow cooking.

MRS. MARGARET JENNINGS. La Conner.

Cranberry Pudding.

The dumpling dough: Sift one cup flour with one teaspoon baking powder, pinch of salt; wet with milk and stir with a fork; turn on moulding board and shape with a fork into a ring.

One quart of cranberries, one-half as much sugar as berries, one-half as much water as sugar. Put part of the berries in pudding dish, add part of sugar; lay the dough in a ring on the berries; add the rest of the berries, sugar and water. Cover closely and let cook about ten minutes after beginning to cook.

Turn out on large plate and serve with cream, whipped or plain. MRS. J. J. L.

Date Pudding.

One cup suet chopped fine; beat the suet and one cup sugar together with the yolks of two eggs until light; add one cup milk, three cups flour, one teaspoon cinnamon, one-half teaspoon nutmeg, the beaten whites of two eggs, one teaspoon baking powder (in flour), one-half pound each of chopped raisins and dates. Put into greased mould and steam three hours.

MRS. M. DENEHIE, Bellingham.

Apple Dumplings.

Make a very rich biscuit dough to the amount you will require. Pare and slice firm, sour apples—it is well to put them in a chopping bowl and chop them, as they are easier to put in the dumplings. Roll out the dough, heap the chopped apple on it and put three tablespoons of sugar to each dumpling and a little cinnamon, bring the edges of the dough together. Do not make them too large, about the size of a cup is good. Put them into a baking pan, strew bits of butter over them and a cup of boiling water. It is well not to have the oven too hot, as it will take some time for the apples to cook through.

Apple Fritters.

For six people take two cups of sweet milk, two well-beaten eggs, a little salt and enough flour to make a smooth, thin batter. Pare and slice four large apples, put this into the batter. Drop by tablespoonfuls into a deep vessel containing hot fat; fry a rich brown. Serve after dipping into powdered sugar, as an accompaniment to a meat course, or with maple syrup as a dessert.

Strawberry Dumplings.

Into a pint of sifted flour rub two rounded tablespoonfuls of butter, add one teaspoonful of salt, one egg well beaten, one heaping teaspoonful of baking powder and sufficient milk to moisten. Mix quickly and roll out into a thin sheet about a quarter of an inch thick. Cut out with a round biscuit cutter, place four berries in the center of each, fold the edges over and steam about twenty-five minutes. Serve with strawberry sauce.

MISS MARTHA JENNINGS, La Conner.

Sago Pudding.

Three-fourths cup of sago well washed and cooked in water, then put pie plant or cherries one inch thick in a pudding dish or a granite basin, turn the sago over it and bake a half hour. Sweeten and salt the sago to taste before putting it in the baking dish.

MRS. FRANK CURTIS.

Corn Pudding.

One can corn, two eggs beaten light, one-half cup cracker crumbs, one cup sweet milk, salt and sugar to taste. Bake thirty minutes.   MRS. B. R. McCLELLAND, Olympia.

Baked Apples.

Split the apples in half from blossom to stem; remove the core; place cut side down on a thin layer of sugar in a granite iron pan. Pour on just enough hot water to dissolve the sugar. Bake in a moderately hot oven until the apple is soft. The dissolved sugar is all drawn up into the apple and makes it delicious.

VASHTI BOWERS Seattle.

Prune Whip.

Wash a pint of prunes, then put to soak in hot water; soak as long as you have time, over night is better. Boil slowly until tender in same water. Remove from fire and sweeten to taste, while hot, but don't stew sugar with prunes as it makes them tough.

Press through sieve, colander or anything that will remove skins and seeds, as you only want the pulp. Beat whites of three eggs stiff, then whip the prune pulp in gradually. Beat up well and bake twenty minutes in a baking dish. When cold turn out in a berry dish, on which has been poured one-half pint of sweetened and flavored cream.

MRS. A. L. CALLOW, Elma.

Orange Pudding.

Six oranges sliced thin, sprinkled with one-half cupful sugar. Make the following custard: One pint milk, two tablespoons sugar, yolks of three eggs. Cook in a double boiler. When cold pour over the oranges. Whip whites of eggs stiff; add two tablespoons sugar and spread over custard.

Steamed Bread Pudding.

One quart bread crumbs, one cup flour, one cup milk, one cup molasses, one cup raisins or currants, two eggs, one teaspoon soda, one-half teaspoon each of cinnamon and nutmeg, pinch of salt. Steam three or four hours.

Cornstarch Pudding.

Put in a double boiler a scant quart sweet milk, add three tablespoons sugar. Heat to near boiling. Beat two eggs, a little cold milk and four tablespoons cornstarch. Stir briskly into the hot milk and cook a few minutes. When partly cool add flavoring to taste. Serve with cream and sugar or fruit sauce.

E. H. STRUZENBERG, Avon.

Steamed Carrot Pudding.

There are many different recipes for plum pudding, but this carrot pudding takes the place of one and is not too rich. One egg, one cup sugar, one cup finely chopped suet, one cup grated carrot, one cup grated potato, one cup raisins, one cup currents floured, one cup citron cut fine, two cups flour, one-half teaspoon salt, also cinnamon, allspice and nutmeg. Mix one teaspoon soda in the grated potato and stir all the ingredients together. Steam three hours. This makes a good-sized pudding. Serve with a good sauce.

MRS. EMMA ALLEN, Avon.

Tapioca Pudding.

Boil two cups of tapioca in three pints of water until clear. Then add two cups of sugar and four oranges sliced and the juice of one lemon. Boil for two minutes. Let cool, then add two whites of eggs, well beaten, and put in a cool place. Serve with whipped cream. Any preserved fruit can be used instead of oranges.

MRS. O. OFFERDAHL, Seattle.

Custard Pudding.

One pint sweet milk, one cup sifted flour, stir together and cook until thick. When it is cool stir in four beaten eggs, two cups sugar and one cup chopped citron. Bake until it sets; serve cold with or without sauce.

EDNA MERCHANT, Avon.

Rice Custard.

One pint milk, one-fourth cup rice, two tablespoons sugar, one teaspoon vanilla, one-half pint cream, one tablespoon gelatine. Put milk and rice on to boil in double boiler, cook one hour. Soak gelatine in cold water and pour the boiling rice on it; stir well, then let cool. Next beat a little with the egg beater and put in sugar and vanilla. Whip the cream and stir slowly into the mixture. Beat with the egg beater until light, pour in a mold, set in a cool place until firm. Serve with whipped cream.

MRS. CLARA SAUERS, Aberdeen.

Mountain Dew.

One pint milk, scant, three-fourths cup rolled crackers, one-fourth cup sugar, one large cup of shredded cocoanut, yolks of two eggs. Make meringue of the whites and set in oven to brown; add a little milk if needed.

MRS. CARRIE N. OAKLEY, Anacortes.

Caramel Custard.

Melt one-half cup sugar to light brown. One pint hot milk added slowly; when cool add the yolks of four eggs and the whites of two; flavor with vanilla. Bake like the usual custard.

Make a meringue of the whites of two eggs beaten with four tablespoons of sugar and spread on top when baked. Return to oven and brown slightly.

MISS ROSALIE KELLOGG, Portland, Ore.

Custard Pudding.

A good rule for custard pudding is seven eggs to two quarts of milk, and about five tablespoons of sugar. Flavoring.

This is a good foundation for many puddings. A cup of bread crumbs makes it into bread custard, and the addition of half a cup of raisins makes still another variety of dessert.

When baking a custard the pudding dish should always be put in another dish of water in the oven; this will produce even baking.

Chess Cake or Transparent Custard.

(Old fashioned Southern recipe.)

Three eggs, three cups sugar, one-half cup butter. Heat thoroughly and flavor; line three ordinary pie tins with pie crust and put the above amount into them. Bake in a very slow oven at least one-half hour, and set in cool place to become firm.

FANNY LEAKE CUMMINGS, M. D., Seattle.

Blackberry Pudding.

Butter thin slices of bread (with the crusts cut off) on both sides; put a layer of the buttered bread in a deep dish, then a layer of blackberries, either fresh or canned, and so on until the dish is filled. Cover the top with sugar and a sprinkling of cinnamon.

Better made twenty-four hours before eating. Serve with whipped cream, or if that is not to be had with thin sweet cream.

MRS. FLORA A. P. ENGLE, Coupeville.

Fruit Gelatine.

To one quart of pure fruit juice, grape or blackberry preferred, add one-half package of gelatine. Set away over night to mold and serve with cream, or, better still, with whipped cream.

MRS. ANNA B. MEYER, Seattle.

Blackberry Pandowdy.

One quart of blackberries in a buttered pudding dish, one cup flour in another bowl, with one and one-half teaspoons of baking powder, one salt spoon of salt and a tablespoon of butter; rub up fine.

Beat yolks of two eggs with one cup of milk and one tablespoon of sugar, add to flour, stirring to a smooth batter. Beat whites of eggs to a stiff froth and add to batter, then pour the batter over the berries and bake in a moderately quick oven. Serve with hot or cold sauce.

SARAH KENDALL, M. D., Seattle.

Banana Whip.

Put six bananas through a fruit press, whip whites of two eggs with four tablespoons of sugar; beat this into the bananas. Put in ice chest in dishes in which it is to be served; cut pineapple in dice and place three or four pieces on top of each dish, then a spoonful of whipped cream, topped with a strawberry.

MRS. I. E. SHRANGER, Mt. Vernon.

Marshmellow Gelatine.

One pound of marshmellows cut into dice, pour over this one can of grated pineapple. Put on ice over night; serve with whipped cream.

MRS. C. F. ZIMMERMAN, Seattle.

Almond Parfait.

Boil one-half cup sugar in one-half cup water without stirring, until it reaches the soft ball stage. Pour over the beaten whites of two eggs, beat until cold, add quarter pound of shredded almonds, 1 tablespoon lemon juice and half a pint of stiff whipped cream. Pour in mould and bury in ice and salt for four hours.

Pineapple Charlotte.

One quart of cream, one-half box of gelatine, one-half pound of sugar, one teaspoon of vanilla, half teaspoon of orange extract, half pint of solid cooked pineapple.

Whip the cream until stiff. When very stiff add the sugar, flavoring and pineapple. Take the gelatine, which has been soaked in cold water and pour over it one small cup boiling water, boil one minute; remove and let stand until nearly cold. Pour it into the cream and stir continuously until cold, or the gelatine will settle. Stand in a cold place.

MRS. NEAL CALKINS, La Conner.

Fruit Cocktail.

This makes a very appetizing first course and may be served at a breakfast, dinner or luncheon. Use as many different fruits as possible. To serve six persons, peel and cut into dice two oranges, one-half pineapple—canned may be used—two plums, two pears or any other fruit that will not discolor by standing. Put over this one cup sugar, and at serving time mix two bananas, two peaches, cubes of melon, red and white grapes may be added. Serve in tall goblets. Oranges, pineapple, bananas and red and white grapes make a good combination.

MRS. CLARA SAUERS, Aberdeen.

Ambrosia.

Three large oranges, six bananas, one small can pineapple. Peel oranges; chip into a dish a layer, then a layer of the banana and same of the pineapple, then sugar to taste. Put in alternate layer until all are used, adding lastly the pineapple juice. This is very fine.

MARIA HAYS McHENRY, Olympia.

Fruit Juice Jelly.

Soak one box gelatine in two cups of cold water for half an hour; add one quart of boiling water, in which a stick of cinnamon has been cooked. Stir until dissolved; add one pint of fruit juice (any kind desired), one and a half pounds of sugar and the juice of two lemons. Strain into moulds and set away to harden.

MRS. HELEN GRINDALL, Seattle.

Orange Gelatine.

One-half package of gelatine soaked in one-half cup cold water, one cup sugar, juice of one lemon, juice and pulp of two oranges, one and one-half quarts of boiling water. Set away in cold place until stiff.

Mock Cantaloupe.

Line tin melon mould with lady fingers; make custard with beaten yolks of two eggs, one-half cup of sugar beaten well together, heat one cup of sweet milk and pour on eggs and sugar. Put in double boiler and cook until mixture clings to spoon. Take three scant tablespoon of Knox gelatine dissolved in one-quarter cup of cold water, pour hot custard over gelatine and set until cold; then add one cup of cream whipped stiff; stir well and pour into mould, cover with lady fingers, put on ice for three hours.

Have Pistachio nuts chopped fine; take from mould carefully to platter, sprinkle thickly with the chopped nuts; stack whipped cream around and serve.

MRS. J. C. HAINES, Seattle.

Marshmallow Cream.

Whip one pint of cream to a stiff froth. Take one pound of marshmallows and cut each into four pieces; add to the cream and beat thoroughly. Place in a refrigerator until chilled. Then serve in individual dishes, sprinkling chopped walnuts over the top.

Banana Charlotte.

Soak one-quarter box of pulverized gelatine in one-quarter cup of cold water. Chill and whip one pint of cream; sprinkle over the cream one-half cup of powdered sugar and one teaspoon orange extract. Dissolve gelatine in a half cup boiling water and when cool strain it into the cream and whip. When nearly stiff, pour into two pint moulds, which have been lined with bananas, peeled, cut in halves lengthwise and shaped to the depth of the moulds.

Velvet Cream.

Beat stiff the whites of two eggs, add two tablespoonfuls of powdered sugar and four tablespoonfuls of jelly (always two different kinds of jelly, blackberry and currant make a good combination), beat to a cream. Then whip cream and fill individual glasses half full of the whipped cream and finish filling the glass with the jelly cream.

Strawberries in Cream.

One-half box of gelatine dissolved in one-half cup of cold water, add to it three cupfuls of boiling water, one cupful of sugar and the juice of two lemons. Stir well and strain. Put away to set (it will be only one-half as stiff as most jellies). Mix a cupful of whipped cream with one quart of nice strawberries, previously sweetened, and stir very carefully into the gelatine that is already set. Fill custard glasses nearly full and on top of each put a spoon of whipped cream.

Peach Dessert.

Pare and mash fine the amount of peaches that you think you will require. Put the peaches in a glass dish and cover with one-half pint of whipped cream in which has been stirred one cup of powdered sugar; set away on ice to chill. Sprinkle chopped almonds on top when you serve.

Spanish Cream.

Pour half a pint of milk over half a box of gelatine and let stand long enough to thoroughly dissolve. Put a scant quart of milk into a double boiler and let come to a boil. Then stir the dissolved gelatine into the hot milk. Beat well the yolks of three eggs and add six tablespoons of sugar and half a cupful of milk; mix well before stirring into the hot milk. One teaspoonful of vanilla for flavoring.

Put the whites of three eggs beaten very stiff in the bottom of the mold, and pour the whole mixture into the same and the whites of the eggs will come to the top. Set away in a cold place to harden. When the cream is turned out of the mold it will present a very pretty appearance, as the clear gelatine will be at the bottom, the yellow custard in the middle, and on top the layer of white.

Serve with cream, whipped or not as preferred.

Raspberry Cream.

Dissolve one teaspoonful of gelatine in about a quarter of a cupful of cold water and pour over it a quarter of a cupful of boiling water. Take one pint of cream and flavor with vanilla and a cupful of raspberry juice, sweeten with three tablespoonfuls of sugar. Pour into this the dissolved gelatine and beat well with an egg-beater. Put into a tight mold and pack in ice and rock-salt for two hours. This should be stiff so that you could serve it the same as brick ice cream.

Strawberry Parfait.

Beat stiff the whites of two eggs; heat a cupful of strawberry jam or jelly over the fire until hot, then beat gradually into it the whites of the eggs. Whip until cool; flavor with a tablespoonful of lemon juice and vanilla. Set aside to get cold, then whip in two cupfuls of thick cream beaten stiff.

Put into a mold and pack in ice and salt four hours. Turn out and serve with whipped cream. A few fresh berries makes a pretty garnish.

Muskmelons With Ice Cream.

Use carefully selected melons; wash and put away on ice for several hours. Cut in halves and remove the seeds; fill each half with ice cream. Chopped nuts may be sprinkled over the top.

Many additional fruits may be used in combination. Dot the top with fresh strawberries or cubes of pineapple.

Halved peaches or pears chilled and served with ice cream are very delicious.

Luncheon Parfait.

Boil one cupful of sugar and one-half cupful of water to the soft ball stage and gradually whip it into the beaten whites of three eggs; continue whipping until cold. Use one scant teaspoonful of violet extract for flavoring, and fold into it a pint of stiffly beaten cream. Pour into a mold and pack in salt and ice four or five hours. Serve with whipped cream and a border of candied violets.

Very dainty and appropriate for a spring luncheon.

Strawberry Mousse.

Mash well together one quart of thick rich cream, one pound of fine granulated sugar and one quart of ripe strawberries; rub strawberries and sugar through a sieve. Dissolve half a box of gelatine in a cup of cold water and set in a place where it will warm gradually.

Whip the cream to a stiff froth; pour in the dissolved gelatine and continue whipping with the pan set in ice, and add gradually the fruit juice.

Cranberry Bavarian Cream.

Soak a tablespoonful of gelatine in cold water and then

dissolve by pouring over it a cupful of hot water; add to it a cupful of sugar; let cool. Whip a pint of cream stiff and mix with it the gelatine. Keep the bowl containing the mixture in a pan of cracked ice, and when the cream begins to stiffen stir in one cupful of cranberry juice made very sweet and mixed with the juice of one lemon. Turn into a tight covered mold and pack in salt and ice for about five hours.

Strawberry Float.

Mash well two quarts of strawberries and beat into them the beaten whites of four eggs and a cupful of sugar. Beat until very light and foamy; turn into serving dish and set away on ice to chill.

Banana Custard.

Three bananas, one pint of boiling water, two tablespoonfuls of butter, three-quarters of a cupful of sugar, the whites of four eggs, five level tablespoonfuls of cornstarch and half a cupful of orange juice. Cut the bananas into half inch blocks. Pour the orange juice over them to improve the flavor and to prevent them from turning dark. Set them aside and stir occasionally. Put the cornstarch and sugar into a saucepan, mix thoroughly, then pour on the boiling water and stir constantly over the fire until the mixture boils and clears; then add the butter. Stir until it melts. Fold lightly in the whites of the eggs, which have been beaten to a stiff froth and remove from the fire. Mix in the bananas and orange juice. Turn into a serving dish and set away to become very cold. Serve with cream.

Fruit Tapioca Pudding.

Boil one-half cupful of pearl tapioca in one quart of boiling water until soft and transparent. Add one-half teaspoonful of salt and one-half cupful of sugar. Pare and core three large tart apples and three pears and fill the centers with sugar and a clove; put in baking dish and pour tapioca around them. Bake until the fruit is tender. Serve hot or cold with cream and sugar.

Christmas Sherbet.

One dozen blood oranges, one quart of water, one pint of sugar. Peel the oranges, cut in halves across the sections, remove the seeds and press out the juice; add the sugar and water, and when the sugar is dissolved strain into the can and freeze.

Strawberry Sherbet.

Peel a banana and cut in thin slices, peel an orange and remove the sections, discarding all seeds and membranes; cut two or three thin slices of pineapple in dice, remove the seeds and skins from a cupful of white grapes and add a pint of strawberries; sprinkle with powdered sugar, mix thoroughly and set aside, buried in ice, until well chilled.

Boil one pint of water and one and one-half cupfuls of sugar ten minutes; add half a teaspoonful of gelatine softened in a teaspoonful of cold water, and strain into the can of the freezer.

When cold add one pint of the strawberry juice and freeze as usual. Serve the chilled fruit in glasses, a spoonful of sherbet on the top of each glass. The juice of any fruit may be used, or the juice of several fruits. Half a cupful each of pineapple, orange, strawberry and currant, with the juice of one lemon, will be found nice.

Cranberry Sherbet.

Boil one quart of cranberries in one pint of water until very soft; strain through a sieve and add two cups of granulated sugar; also the juice of two lemons and one tablespoonful of gelatine previously soaked in a little cold water and dissolve in hot water. Freeze to a mush in the usual way.

This makes a delightful change from the usual cranberry sauce on the Thanksgiving table.

Fruit Sherbet.

Use one cupful each of raspberry, pineapple and currant juice (ther erae many other delightful combinations such as blackberry, currant and strawberry), one-half cupful of lemon juice. Add as much water as fruit juice and sweeten very sweet as it will be less sweet when frozen. Freeze in the usual way.

Grape Sherbet.

Boil one pound of sugar with one quart of water for five minutes. Pulp three pounds of Concord grapes; add the pulp and the skins to the syrup and stand aside to get cold. When cold put through a fine seive, being careful not to mash the seeds. Freeze, but not too stiff.

Frozen Cherries.

Some prefer the dark cherries, but the Royal Ann are also very nice this way. Pit carefully and sprinkle with plenty of sugar; pour into tightly covered mold and pack in salt and ice for several hours. Nice to serve with cake for luncheons. May be garnished with whipped cream.

Strawberry and Lemon Ice.

To one quart of strawberries add a pint of water and a pound of sugar. Let boil about twenty minutes. Then add the juice of two lemons. Strain through a sieve that is fine enoughh to exclude the seeds. Freeze. This will be found very delicious.

Mixed Fruit Sorbet.

A pint of water and a pint of sugar boiled together for five minutes. When cold and ready to freeze, add two cupfuls of currant juice, one cupful of orange juice, one finely shredded pineapple and freeze to a mush.

Ginger Water Ice.

This will require one quart of lemon water ice and six ounces of preserved ginger. Pound four ounces of the ginger to a paste. The remaining two ounces cut into small dice; stir all into the water ice. Repack and stand away to ripen.

Pineapple Desserts.

Pineapple Sponge.

Peel and chop fine one small pineapple. Put it with the juice into a saucepan with a cupful of sugar and a cupful of water. Simmer ten minutes; soak half a package of gelatine in a half cupful of water for two hours. Add to the sweetened pineapple and strain into a bowl. When nearly cold add the whites of four eggs and beat until the mixture begins to thicken; then pour into a mould and set to harden. Serve with whipped cream.

Pineapple Float.

Beat the whites of four eggs ten minutes; add four tablespoonfuls of sugar; pour over a cupful of pineapple pulp and mix carefully; set on ice until thoroughly chilled; serve in individual glass plates with whipped cream piled on top.

Pineapple Parfait.

Boil a cupful of sugar and half a cupful of water to the soft ball stage. Pour on the whites of two eggs beaten until foamy; then beat until cold. Fold in the whip from two cupfuls of cream and one cupful of shredded pineapple. Turn into a mold and bury in ice and salt for two hours.

Pineapple Souffle.

After paring a pineapple, cut in small pieces, add one cupful of sugar and cook until clear. Mix two tablespoons of cornstarch with a little cold water and stir into the cooked pineapple; add the juice of half a lemon and the whites of three eggs beaten stiff. Fill baking cups with the mixture, bake in a pan of water twenty minutes. Serve with sweet, foamy sauce.

Pineapple Delight.

Take a large pineapple, cut off the top and square the bottom so that it will stand firm. Scoop out the pulp with a strong spoon; save the pulp but discard the tough core.

Pare several oranges, divide into sections and cut into small pieces; stem a few strawberries, pit a few cherries, slice peaches, plums, apricots or any other fruit to be found in the market; mix the pineapple pulp and the other fruits, add the juice of a lemon and powdered sugar to sweeten; place on ice for an hour longer and when ready to serve fill into the chilled shell of the pineapple and garnish as fancy may dictate.

Pineapple and Strawberry Dessert.

Take large, sweet strawberries, chop pineapple coarsely and put in a glass dish alternate layers of strawberries and chopped pineapple; sweeten and pour over it a cupful of orange juice. Set away on ice to harden, or rather to chill, and serve with or without cream, as preferred.

Turkish Pineapple Cream.

Shred a pineapple with a silver fork and mix with one cupful of powdered sugar; add a pint of cream whipped very stiff and one ounce of gelatine dissolved in a little water. Pour the mixture into a melon mold that has been previously oiled. Pack in ice and salt for two hours.

Gooseberry Pudding.

Fill an earthen or granite ware baking dish nearly full of stemmed gooseberries and add sugar—plenty of it—and a little water. Put into a bowl one cupful of buttermilk and add a teaspoonful each of soda and salt, one tablespoonful of lard or butter, and stir in flour to make a batter stiff enough to spread smoothly over the fruit; bake in a moderate oven.

Serve with sweet cream.

Strawberry Sponge Roll.

Before making your roll wash two quarts of berries and drain them; slice across the berries, making two or three slices according to the size of the berries; sprinkle with granulated sugar, using one cupful of sugar. Reserve the best berries to serve a few with each slice of the roll.

For the roll beat the yolks of three eggs until stiff, then add gradually a quarter of a pound of granulated sugar; place on the back of the stove where it is warm but not hot, and beat well for fifteen minutes. Flavor with vanilla extract to taste.

Sift a quarter of a pound of flour and stir in slowly, but

do not beat any more. Pour the latter to the depth of a third of an inch in flat biscuit pans and bake in a hot oven, lining the pans with buttered paper. Do not bake too brown. Spread the fruit on the cake while the latter is warm and roll up quickly, taking off the paper as you roll. When rolled wrap the cake tightly in a napkin and as soon as it will keep in shape serve with sweet cream.

Pastry

"Male and female created He them, and gave them dominion over the earth."

English Mince Meat.

Cook two pounds of lean meat in a little salted water until tender. Chop finely as possible. Add one pound of shredded suet, four pounds of peeled, cored and chopped apples, five cups of sugar, two pounds of currants, two pounds of raisins, one grated nutmeg, one-half teaspoon of mace, the grated rind and juice of six oranges and two lemons, one-half cup of juice of any kind of fruit preserves, four tablespoons of vinegar, one tablespoon of salt. This is fine.

W. E. CHAMBERLIN, Olympia.

Rhubarb Pie.

One cup chopped rhubarb, one egg, one cup sugar, scant half cup water, one cracker rolled fine, grated rind of one lemon. Bake with top crust.

MRS. I. E. SCHRANGER, Mt. Vernon.

Cream Lemon Pie.

Grate the rind of a lemon and squeeze out the juice, one cup sugar, one tablespoon of butter, one tablespoon of flour, yolks of two eggs; beat well, then add one cup of milk or cream—cream is best—then the beaten whites of the eggs beaten in last. Put in shell and bake.

MRS. G. F. ZIMMERMAN, Seattle.

Lemon Pie—One Pie.

Grated rind and juice of one lemon, one cup of sugar, one cup of bread crumbs, three eggs, use the yolks and one white, one-half cup of hot water. Use the remaining two whites for a meringue for the top.

MRS. I. E. SHRANGER, Mt. Vernon.

Pumpkin Pie—One Pie.

One cup stewed and mashed pumpkin or squash, one cup sweet milk, one cup sugar, one egg, one tablespoon molasses, one teaspoon each of ginger, cinnamon and allspice.

MRS. SUSAN GRIFFITH, Bellingham.

Blackberry Pie.

Line a deep pie dish with crust, then fill it with ripe blackberries; mix together one cup of sugar and tablespoon of flour, pour this over the berries, dust with cinnamon and cover with top crust. Rub a teaspoon of cream over crust before putting in the oven; a rich brown when baked.

The above recipe will answer for all fresh berry pies. Very sour berries, as gooseberries, will require more sugar and sweet berries less. Some cooks prefer to stew the berries before putting in the pie, but the flavor of the fruit is certainly finer if put into the pie raw.

Apple Pie.

Pare and slice very thin, firm, sour apples—perhaps Gravenstein apples in their season make the best apple pies. Line your pie dish with pastry and fill heaping full with the sliced apples; pour over this one cup sugar and a half teaspoon of cinnamon; do not add any water. Cover with crust. Delicious.

MRS. MARGARET JENNINGS.

Cocoanut Custard Pie.

Two eggs, two cups milk, one-half cup sugar, half teaspoon of vanilla. Pour this custard into a pie dish lined with pastry and sprinkle carefully over the top a teacup of shredded cocoanut. Bake in a slow oven.

MRS. ADDA HURLBERT GACHES, La Conner.

Custard Pie.

Crust—One cup of flour, one big tablespoon of lard, one small lump of butter, pinch of salt, one-half teaspoon sugar, one-half teaspoon baking powder and enough hot water to make stiff dough; roll thin. Use only one crust.

For each pie take the yolks of three eggs well beaten and add one and one-half cups of milk, one-half cup sugar, mix well and bake in a moderate oven until light brown. Beat the three whites and put on top. Then place in oven for a few minutes until light brown.

MRS. O. OFFERDAHL.

Lemon Pie—Reliable.

Grated rind and juice of one lemon, one cup of white sugar, two cups of boiling water, one-half cup of flour, two eggs. Put lemon and water on stove, mix the sugar and flour together while dry, then use enough water to make a rather stiff batter, add the yolks of two eggs, when well beaten, stir this mixture into the boiling lemon and water and stir constantly until it thickens.

Have pie tins lined with paste, and well pricked to prevent the crust from puffing; let the crust bake while the filling is cooking. When done fill the pie dish and spread over the top the whites of two eggs beaten to a stiff froth with three teaspoons of sugar added gradually. Set in oven on grate and bake to a light cream color. This will insure a good, firm lemon pie.

MRS. SUSAN GRIFFITH, Bellingham.

Cream Pie.

One pint milk, yolks of two eggs, two tablespoons cornstarch, one-half cup sugar. Use whites as meringue for top.

MRS. SUSAN GRIFFITH, Bellingham.

Banana Pie.

Make a lower crust and bake. Take two-thirds cup of milk and two-thirds cup cream, one egg, one-third cup sugar, one tablespoon flour, flavor with vanilla. Pour the filling into the crust, slice a banana into the pie, when you have poured it about half-full of the filling. Frost the top with the white of an egg.

MISS ROSE OSBERG, La Conner.

Vinegar Pie.

One scant cup sugar, one egg, two tablespoons good vinegar, one heaping tablespoon flour, one scant cup water, flavor with nutmeg, beat all together. Bake with two crusts.

MRS. ANNIE E. TAYLOR.

Mock Cherry Pie.

One large cup cranberries, one cup raisins, cut in halves, three tablespoons flour, one cup sugar, two cups water. Boil cranberries with the two cups of water until soft; add raisins, sugar, flour and two teaspoons of vanilla. May need more water. Makes two pies. Bake like any fruit pie.

MRS. D. R. TOMLIN, Kirkland.

Squash Pie.

Cut squash in small pieces, cook in a little water slowly until done. For one pie allow: One and one-half cups squash, one cup boiling milk, one teaspoon butter, one-half cup sugar, one-half teaspoon salt, cinnamon, nutmeg, ginger, one egg beaten separately. Half bake crust, fill with mixture, bake until it puffs up.

MRS. OAKLEY, Anacortes.

Ripe Currant Pie.

One cup of currants, mash well, three-fourths cup of sugar and one teaspoon of flour (mix flour and sugar together), one egg. Mix the egg with currants and sugar and bake with two crusts.

MRS. FLORA A. P. ENGLE, Coupeville.

Cakes

"Properly understood, suffrage does not mean the appointing of ward heelers; it means the park system, the public schools, the hospitals, play-grounds and public libraries. In matters of this kind we make no distinction between men and women. Today, to secure the best results in city government, we must have the common service of men and women."

Chocolate Frosting.

One cup sugar, one-half cup water, cream of tartar size of a bean, boil until it spins a thread. When cool add butter size of an almond, and stir to a cream, first adding grated chocolate to taste and teaspoon of vanilla.

MRS. HATTIE B. DUNLAP, Mt. Vernon.

Frosting.

Take one tablespoonful of good rich milk and mix thoroughly with one cup pulverized sugar, flavor to taste and spread on cake.

MRS. GEORGE B. SMITH, Anacortes.

Dry Frosting.

As soon as a loaf cake is removed from pan rub lightly over top one-fourth cup of powdered sugar. Then heat slightly, melting the sugar will cause it to adhere to the cake, making a quick and very acceptable substitute for icing.

LINDA JENNINGS, La Conner.

Boiled Icing.

One cup of sugar, four tablespoons of water. Let it boil until it spins a hair. White of one egg beaten to a stiff froth. Add boiling syrup slowly and whip three minutes.

MRS. IDA A. KEENE, Seattle.

Chocolate Icing.

Perhaps some have experienced difficulty in getting

chocolate smoothly into boiled icing. The following is an original and sure recipe:

One scant cup of sugar, one-third cup water, boil until it hairs. Beat stiff the whites of two eggs; mix two tablespoons of grated chocolate or cocoa with two spoons of sugar. Whip this into the whites, then pour over this slowly the boiled sugar, beating in usual manner. A very fine grained icing is the result.

MADGE JENNINGS, La Conner.

Chocolate Filling.

One cup sugar, two tablespoons chocolate, one-half cup milk (mix sugar and chocolate together while dry); cook until it drops thickly off the spoon. Beat well until it is cool enough to spread. Flavor with vanilla.

MISS CORA SEABERRY.

Caramel Filling.

One cup sugar, two tablespoons cocoa, mixed together, dry butter size of a walnut, one-half cup milk. Cook until it drops thick from the spoon. Spread between the layers before it is quite cold.

MRS. W. J. WALDRIP, Coupeville.

Caramel Filling.

Two cups brown sugar (scant), one-half cup butter (very scant), one-half cup milk. Boil until it is thick, add vanilla and beat a very little.

HARRIET E. WRIGHT, South Bellingham.

Prize Fruit Cake.

Two pounds raisins, two pounds currants, two pounds dates, two pounds figs, two pounds walnuts, two pounds almonds, one pint candied cherries (if liked), one pound sugar, one pound butter, one pound flour, one pound eggs (ten), one-half pint cream, one-quarter pint New Orleans molasses, one-half pint grape juice, one-quarter pint vanilla, one-half pint citron, one ounce each of cinnamon, cloves, allspice and nutmeg.

Cream the butter and sugar, add eggs one at a time. Then add spices and molasses, cream and flour. Prepare for fruit cake the night before by blanching and breaking the almonds. Pour grape juice and vanilla over all fruit and nuts and let stand all night. Pour boiling water over the citron and let stand a few minutes to soften. Mix all together well with the hands, as it is too heavy to stir. Put buttered paper in pans and bake in very moderate oven about four hours. This will keep for years if well wrapped and put away in a stone jar. Not good to eat until at least two weeks old.

MRS. F. W. COTTERILL, Seattle.

Wedding Cake.

One pound of sugar, three-fourths pound of butter creamed together, ten eggs beaten separately, yolks used first, afterward the whites, one-half pound of citron, two pounds of currants rubbed dry in flour, two pounds of raisins, seeded and chopped, two pounds of raisins seeded and left whole, one-half nutmeg, one teaspoon each of cinnamon and cloves, one-fourth cup of sweet milk, one pound of flour sifted and mixed with one teaspoonful baking soda and one teaspoonful of baking powder. Stir in the flour and whole raisins alternately. Line your baking pan with paper and make a paper cap for the top. Bake two hours, heat to be decreased the last hour. Ten cents' worth of blanched almonds shaved fine and one-half pound of citron added will help this.

MRS. F. A. P. ENGLE, Coupeville.

Mahogany Cake.

One cup grated chocolate, one-half cup sweet milk cooked until smooth and creamy, set aside to cool; one and one-half cups sugar, one-half cup butter, three eggs, one-half cup milk, two cups flour, one level teaspoon soda; add cooked chocolate and bake in three or four layers.

Filling.

One and one-half cups sugar, one-half cup sweet milk, butter size walnut, pinch of soda; cook until mixture will hair, flavor with teaspoon of vanilla and beat until cool enough to spread. This is a delicious and popular cake.

MRS. LOLA FOWLER.

Tilden Cake—Loaf Cake.

One cup butter, two cups sugar, one cup sweet milk, three cups flour, one-half cup cornstarch, four eggs, two rounded teaspoons baking powder, lemon extract.

MRS. GRACE HANSON, Stanwood

Devil's Food Cake.

Two squares of Baker's chocolate grated; add yolk of one egg beaten light and one-half cup cold water; boil until this thickens, take off the stove. Dissolve one-half teaspoon soda in one-half cup of boiling water and add to the above.

Then add one tablespoon butter, one-half teaspoon vanilla, one and one-half cups flour, one teaspoon baking powder, one cup sugar.

Filling—Yolks of two eggs, one square chocolate, four tablespoons water, one-half cup sugar; cook until thick, flavor with vanilla. Ice the cake with white boiled icing. This recipe is enough for a large two-layer cake. If made right the cake and filling will both be, when cold, a rich, dark red, not brown. MRS. ANNA M. COMBES.

Marble Cake.

Light part—Whites of three eggs, one cup sugar, one-half cup butter, one-half cup sweet milk, one and one-half cups flour, one-half cup cornstarch, two teaspoons baking powder. Flavor with lemon.

Dark part—Yolks of three eggs, one cup sugar, one-half cup butter, one-half cup sour milk or cold coffee, one-half teaspoon of all kinds of spices, teaspoon of molasses, two cups flour, one cup currants and raisins mixed.

Drop a spoonful of each kind in a well-buttered cake pan. First the light part, then the dark alternately. Try to drop it in so that the cake shall be well streaked, with the appearance of marble. MRS. DICKSON.

Potato Cake.

Two cups sugar, one cup butter, four eggs, one-half cup sweet milk, one and one-half cups mashed potatoes, one and one-half cups flour, two squares chocolate, one cup chopped walnuts, one teaspoon each of cinnamon, nutmeg and cloves, two teaspoons baking powder. Bake as loaf cake or in layers.

The Famous Lady Baltimore Cake.

One pound finely sifted granulated sugar, one-half pound butter, one pound flour, four teaspoons baking powder, seven eggs, one teaspoon almond essence, one cup sweet milk. Cream sugar and butter, beat in yolks of the eggs, add the flour sifted with the baking powder alternately with the cup of milk, add teaspoon almond essence and lastly the stiffly beaten whites of the eggs. Frosting to suit. This recipe has often been sold for five dollars.

MARIA HAYS-McHENRY, Olympia.

Devil's Food.

Two cups dark brown sugar, one-half cup butter, two eggs, one-half cup sour milk, three cups flour, pinch of salt, mix thoroughly. Into one-half cup of boiling water stir one teaspoon soda and one-half cup grated chocolate or Baker's cocoa; mix with batter.

Filling—Two cups dark brown sugar, one-half cup butter, one-half cup sweet milk or cream; cook until it thickens.

MRS. JENNIE DAVIDSON, Orting.

Silver Cake.

Two cups sugar, three-fourths cup butter, one cup milk, whites of five eggs beaten very stiff, three and one-half cups of sifted flour, vanilla, two teaspoons baking powder. Cream the butter and sugar, mix in the other ingredients, last the beaten whites of the eggs.

This should be a very delicate white cake if properly baked. The addition of a cup of chopped nuts makes a fine nut cake. If nuts are added less butter should be used.

MRS. O. S. JONES, Walla Walla.

Gold Cake.

One cup sugar, one-half cup butter, one cup sweet milk, yolks of five eggs, two teaspoons baking powder, flour to make batter as for the usual loaf cake. Flavor with vanilla.

By adding four tablespoons of cocoa and spice to this recipe it is splendid as the dark part of marble cake. Use the silver cake above for the light part.

MRS. O. S. JONES, Walla Walla.

Silver Cake.

(Without milk or baking powder.)

One pound flour, one pound sugar, one-fourth pound butter, sixteen eggs (use whites only).

Beat whites of eggs to stiff froth; cream butter and sugar together and add flour and eggs alternately until all is used; flavor to suit. Bake in slow oven for one hour.

Very close-grained and most delicious.

FANNY LEAKE CUMMINGS, M. D.

Gold Cake.

One pound butter, one pound flour, one pound sugar, two-thirds cup sweet milk, one-half teaspoon baking powder, sixteen eggs (yolks only).

Bake same as silver cake.

FANNY LEAKE CUMMINGS, M. D.

Tea Cakes.

Four eggs, one cup sugar, flavoring and enough flour to make batter thin as sponge cake batter.

Grease well a large dripping pan and place small spoonfuls of the batter in the pan, but far enough apart that the cake will not run together as it cooks. When baked, if rightly done, you will have small cakes about the size of a coffee cup; remove carefully and bring the edges of the cake over each other forming a ring like a napkin ring. Do not pile on top of each other and spoil shape. These are very nice when serving light refreshments.

MRS. PETER DOWNEY, La Conner.

Walnut Cake.

Two cups brown sugar, one-half cup butter, one cup sour milk, two cups of flour, one cup nuts, three eggs, one teaspoon soda, cinnamon, cloves and nutmeg to taste, one cup raisins. Chop nuts and raisins together. Bake in slow oven.

MRS. IDA A. KEENE, Seattle.

Caramel Cake.

To be baked in layers. One-half cup butter, one and one-half cups sugar, one cup milk, whites of four eggs, three cups flour, two teaspoons baking powder.

Filling—Yolks of four eggs, one cup water and grated rind and juice of one lemon, two tablespoons cornstarch, three-quarters cup sugar, teaspoon butter. Put filling between cake when cold.

MRS. CARRIE N. OAKLEY, Anacortes.

Potato Caramel Cake.

One cup sugar, one-half cup butter, one-half cup mashed potatoes, one-half cup milk, one-fourth cake chocolate, one-half teaspoon nutmeg, one-half spoon cinnamon, pinch of allspice, two rounding teaspoons baking powder, two eggs, one-half spoon vanilla, one-half cup chopped walnuts, two cups flour. Bake in layers and fill with the following icing: Two cups pulverized sugar, one tablespoon butter, three tablespoons milk, one teaspoon vanilla; beat to a cream and spread between layers.

BESSIE BENSON, Avon.

Prune Cake.

Two eggs well beaten, one cup sugar, one teaspoon cinnamon, one-half teaspoon cloves, one-half teaspoon nutmeg, butter size walnut, pinch of salt, one cup sour milk, two small cups flour, one large teaspoon soda, one and one-half cup stewed prunes, pitted and chopped.

MRS. STELLA MOWREY.

Sunshine Cake.

Whites of seven eggs—small, fresh ones—yolks of five eggs, two-thirds cup pastry flour sifted four times, one cup granulated sugar sifted four times, one-third teaspoon cream tartar, a pinch of salt, flavoring. Throw the salt with the whites of eggs. Beat half and sift cream tartar and beat very stiff. Beat sugar in lightly, using wire egg beater; beat yolks with Dover egg beater and add two tablespoon of beaten whites, fold into the mixture thoroughly, add flavoring and flour. Bake in a moderate oven from thirty-five to forty minutes. When cake springs to the touch of finger and leaves the side of the pan it is done; turn upside down to cool.

NELLIE A. LANGDON, Chicago.

Pork Cake.

One pound salt pork chopped fine, one pound raisins, one pint boiling water, two cups molasses, one tablespoon soda, one tablespoon nutmeg, one tablespoon each cinnamon, cloves and allspice.

MRS. L. M. HALL, Puyallup.

Cream Cake.

Two cups sugar, one-half cup butter, three cups flour, two spoons baking powder, three eggs. Cream the butter and sugar, add eggs one at a time without separating; beat well. Add milk, sift baking powder with flour, then add to the rest and beat well after adding flavoring. Bake in a moderate oven. Filling: Whip one cup cream, putting in sugar and vanilla to taste; sprinkle with cocoanut.

MISS NELLIE DE BOLT, Puyallup.

Apple Sauce Cake.

One and one-half cups apple sauce, one cup sugar, one-half cup butter, one teaspoon soda, stirred in sauce; one teaspoon each cinnamon, allspice, cloves and one cup seeded raisins. Stir all ingredients together on stove until butter is softened, but not melted, then add two cups sifted flour with a teaspoon baking powder and two well-beaten eggs, leaving out the white of one for frosting.

Frosting—One cup sugar, one-half cup water. Boil until it spins a thread, then pour over well-beaten white of egg and beat until as thick as cream.

MRS. J. M. GRIFFITH, Bellingham.

Chocolate Cake.

Beat to a cream half a cup of butter and gradually beat into this one cup sugar. Add one ounce of Baker's premium No. 1 chocolate melted, also two unbeaten eggs. Beat for five minutes, then stir in half a cup of milk, lastly one cup and a half of flour, with which has been mixed one generous teaspoon baking powder. Flavor with one teaspoon vanilla. Pour into a shallow pan and bake for half an hour in a moderate oven. Cover with frosting.

MRS. CARRIE N. OAKLEY Anacortes.

Roll Jelly Cake.

One cup sugar, two eggs beaten separately, two tablespoons milk, one cup flour, two teaspoons baking powder, lemon extract.

MRS. CARRIE N. OAKLEY Anacortes.

White Cake.

One cup granulated sugar, one-half cup butter, two cups flour, two teaspoons baking powder, two-thirds cup sweet milk, whites of three eggs, flavoring.

Cream together the butter and sugar, then add the flour and mix thoroughly with the hands. Add the other ingredients and beat well. MRS. F. M. CLARK.

Sponge Cake.

Five eggs, one and one-half cups granulated sugar, two scant cups sifted flour, one-third cup cold water, two heaping teaspoons baking powder, one-half teaspoon vanilla, salt.

Stir yolks of eggs and sugar until perfectly light, add water, beat whites of eggs and add alternately with flour, mix salt and baking powder in the flour. Bake in a moderate oven.	MRS. B. R. McCLELLAND, Olympia.

Hot Water Sponge Cake.

Four eggs, yolks and whites, beaten separately, add two cups sugar, two cups flour and two heaping teaspoons baking powder, and last three-fourths cup boiling water; stir quickly and well. Bake in four layers in quick oven. Spread layers with whipped cream or an orange filling.
	MRS. LOLA FOWLER.

Layer Cake.

Two cups sugar, one large tablespoon butter, three eggs, one cup milk, three cups flour, two heaping teaspoons baking powder, flavoring to taste. Bake in four layers and serve with any filling desired. The same is very nice, with the addition of rind and juice of half a lemon and baked in a loaf.

White Perfection Cake.

Three cups sugar, one cup butter, one cup milk, three cups flour, one cup cornstarch, whites of twelve eggs beaten very stiff. Two teaspoons cream tartar in flour and one of soda in half the milk. Dissolve cornstarch in remainder of milk and add to sugar and butter well creamed, then milk and soda, flour and whites of eggs.
	MRS. LOLA FOWLER.

Fruit Cake.

One cup butter, one cup sugar, one and one-half cups high-grade molasses, six eggs, six cups flour, two even teaspoons soda, two cups walnuts, two pounds raisins, one pound currants, one teaspoon cinnamon, one-half teaspoon nutmeg, one glass currant jelly.

Citron may be added if desired. Bake two hours or more if necessary.

Rolled Jelly Cake.

Three eggs well beaten, one cup of fine sugar, a pinch of salt, two tablespoons of water, one cup of flour in which there should be one teaspoon of baking powder. The flour to be added gradually.

Bake in a long shallow pan, well greased, in a quick oven. Turn out on a damp towel and cover the top with jelly; roll up while warm.

MRS. E. STRUZENBERG, Avon.

Pecan Nut Cake.

One pound of flour, one pound of sugar, one-third pound of butter, six eggs, one nutmeg, one-half cup of molasses, one and one-half pounds raisins after seeding, one quart of pecans before being cracked, one-half pound of almonds, one tablespoon of baking powder mixed in the flour, one-half cup water. Bake in a moderate oven about three hours. Flour nuts and raisins well.

MRS. LOUISA BERRY, Lexington, Ky.

Coffee Cake.

Two cups brown sugar, one cup butter, four eggs, one cup strong coffee, one teaspoon each of ginger, cloves, cinnamon and nutmeg, three cups flour, one teaspoon of soda and one of baking powder.

MRS. ANDREW OSBERG, La Conner.

Layer Cake.

Two eggs, one cup sugar, three-fourths cup sweet milk, butter size of an egg, two cups flour, one and one-half teaspoons baking powder, flavoring. Use any filling preferred.

MRS. S. A. HUNSICKER, Seattle.

Molasses Layer Cake.

One egg, one-half cup sugar, one-half cup molasses, one-half cup sour milk, butter size of an egg, one teaspoon soda, flour to form a moderately stiff batter.

Filling: Cook one cup chopped raisins with one-half cup of sugar and one-half cup boiling water; boil slowly fifteen minutes; then beat into it the beaten white of an egg. Spread between layers and on top.

MRS. ELMA BENEDICT, Avon.

Eggless Cake.

One cup sugar, one cup sour milk, three scant cups flour, three teaspoons of cocoa, one cup raisins, one-half cup shortening, one teaspoon soda, one teaspoon baking powder, one teaspoon each of cloves, cinnamon and nutmeg. Bake in a loaf in a moderate oven and cover with frosting.

MRS. RHODA A. GIBSON, Avon.

Apple Fruit Cake.

One cup butter, two cups sugar, one cup sweet milk, two eggs, one teaspoon soda, three and one-half cups flour, two cups raisins, two cups of dried apples soaked over night, chopped fine and stewed in two cups of molasses until soft. Beat butter and sugar to a cream, add milk in which dissolve the soda, next the beaten eggs and flour, and lastly stir in the raisins and apples. Season with cloves, nutmegs and cinnamon as for the usual fruit cake.

Bake one and one-half hours.

MRS. JENNIE DAVIDSON, Orting.

Dutch Apple Cake.

Two cups sifted flour, two tablespoons baking powder, salt, one-fourth cup butter, one egg, one cup milk, one-half cup sugar.

Sift dry things together; rub in butter; stir eggs and milk in dry mixture. Spread dought one-half inch thick in pan; cut apples in eighths, lay in rows on top of batter, then sprinkle with sugar and nutmeg. Bake about twenty minutes.

HARRIET E. WRIGHT, South Bellingham.

Rocks.

One and one-half cups sugar, one cup butter, two and one-half cups flour, three eggs well beaten, one small teaspoon soda in a little hot water, one teaspoon cinnamon, a pinch of salt, two cups of seeded raisins, one cup currants, two cups broken walnuts. Drop on buttered tins and bake brown.

MRS. EFFIE B. ROEDER, Bellingham.

Marguerites.

These are very dainty for a luncheon.

The white of an egg beaten for a minute, but not to a stiff froth, two tablespoons of powdered sugar and half a cup of chopped nuts, English walnuts, almonds or pecans, stirred into the egg.

Spread upon long, narrow crackers or upon wafers; set in the oven to brown lightly.

MRS. NELLE MITCHELL FICK, Seattle.

Doughnuts.

Two cups sugar, three eggs, one tablespoon melted butter, one and one-half cups sweet milk, three teaspoons baking powder, little salt, flavor with nutmeg, flour enough to roll.

MRS. ANNIE E. TAYLOR.

Cookie, No. 1.

Four cups of flour, one cup of butter, one and one-half cups sugar, four eggs, two heaping teaspoons baking powder, three tablespoons milk, lemon and nutmeg. Rub butter and flour together, add sugar, beaten eggs, milk and flavoring.

Cookies, No. 2.

Two cups sugar, one full cup butter, one cup buttermilk, two eggs, one teaspoon soda, vanilla, flour to stiffen.

MRS. B. R. McCLELLAND, Olympia.

Oatmeal Cakes.

One tablespoon butter, one cup granulated sugar, stir well, then add two well beaten eggs, one-half cup milk, two cups rolled oats, one teaspoon vanilla, let stand one-half hour then add one cup raisins and one and one-half cups nuts chopped, two cups flour and two teaspoons baking powder.

MRS. ALMA LANGDON.

Oatmeal Crisps (Excellent.)

Two and one-half cups of Quaker rolled oats, one cup sugar, two teaspoons baking powder, one tablespoon melted butter, two eggs, two teaspoons vanilla. Drop mixture one-half teaspoon at a time on buttered pans far apart. Bake ten minutes or more in a moderate oven.

MRS. J. C. HAINES.

Hermits.

Three-fourths cup of shortening, one cup molasses, one cup sugar, two eggs, a large cup sour milk, a teaspoon of soda in a half cup of boiling water. Half a teaspoon each of ginger, nutmeg, cinnamon and cloves. A little salt, three cups of Graham flour, one cup white flour, one cup raisins and half cup finely chopped nuts. Beat well and drop on buttered tins.

Apple Rolls.

Make a rich baking powder biscuit dough, roll out quite thin, spread with apple chopped fine, sprinkle over this some sugar, bits of butter and either cinnamon or nutmeg, roll up like rolled jelly cake and slice off pieces about an inch thick. Place these in a buttered pan and bake a nice brown.

Snowball Doughnuts.

Three eggs, one cup sugar, one tablespoon melted butter, one cup sweet milk, four teaspoons baking powder sifted with flour to roll out. Only one bowl is used in mixing. Beat in each ingredient in order named. Roll one-half inch thick and cut with small baking powder can, cut out center with thimble. Turn often and fry evenly. Dust with sugar in a paper sack.

MRS. S. A. HUNSICKER.

Michigan Doughnuts.

One cup sugar, two eggs, one tablespoon melted lard, one cup hot mashed potatoes, one cup sour milk, one teaspoon soda, one teaspoon baking powder, nutmeg and flour. Mix soft as can be handled and fry in hot cottolene.

MRS. PRUDDEN, Puyallup.

Cream Puffs.

One-half cup butter melted in one cup of hot water. Set on stove to boil, while boiling stir in one cup of flour, stir until smooth. When cool drop in and stir—not beat—one after the other three eggs; drop on hot tins and bake twenty or thirty minutes.

Filling: One cup milk, one egg, one tablespoon sugar. Boil and thicken with cornstarch, flavor with vanilla.

JULIA H. HAWLEY, Kirkland.

Cookies.

Two cups sugar creamed with one cup shortening—cotosuet or cottolene—two eggs, one nutmeg, one teaspoon salt, one full cup milk, three teaspoons baking powder in sieve full of flour. Add flour to roll. Cotosuet or cottolene is better than lard.

MRS. STEVE SMITH.

Rolled Oats Cookies.

Two cups of rolled oats, one and one-half cups sugar, one cup lard, one cup sour milk, nutmeg and cinnamon with flour enough to roll out.

Rocks.

One-half cup butter, one cup sugar, two cups flour, two cups rolled oats, two eggs, five teaspoons sour cream, one teaspoon soda, one cup chopped nuts, half teaspoon each of cinnamon, cloves and allspice, pinch of salt.

Mould with fingers instead of board.

MRS. ANNA HYDE, Seattle.

Brownies.

One-half cup butter, one cup sugar, one-half cup flour, one-half cup nuts chopped, two squares chocolate, two eggs, one teaspoon vanilla. Spread thin in pans; bake in slow oven. Cut in strips when cool.

MRS. ANNA HYDE, Seattle.

Caraway Cookies.

Two cups sugar, one cup butter or the fat skimmed from the top of boiling beef; this is very good, but never use lard. One cup sweet milk, two eggs, two teaspoons baking powder sifted in some of the flour, one small teaspoon caraway seed, little ground nutmeg, mix in enough flour to roll, cut, drop in granulated sugar and bake in quick oven.

Never-Fail Ginger Bread.

One-half cup sugar, one-half cup shortening, one-half cup good molasses, two eggs, one tablespoon ginger, one teaspoon each of cloves and allspice, or nutmeg and cinnamon if liked better, one level teaspoon soda, three cups flour. Smooth lumps out of soda and stir in dry the last thing.

MRS. JENNIE G. CLEGG, Spokane.

Peanut Cookies.

Four tablespoons butter, one beaten egg, two tablespoons milk, lemon extract, salt, four tablespoons sugar, one teaspoon baking powder, eight tablespoons flour, one cup mashed peanuts browned to a crisp. Drop stiff batter into a dripping pan with a teaspoon.

Belgian Hare Ginger Bread.

For the good of the human race, I give you my ginger bread recipe, as I believe every man, woman or child who has reached the age of discrimination will be able to taste it for centuries after. So have it written on parchment made out of a Belgian's skin to better preserve it, and make it for your next Belgian hare dinner.

One cup dark molasses, one-half cup butter, one-half cup sweet milk, two cups flour, two eggs, two teaspoons yeast powder, one tablespoon ginger, one teaspoon allspice. Beat whites and yolks separately.

HAZEL H. HALL.

Egg Bakkelse—Egg Cookies.

Beat three eggs well, and one small tablespoon of sugar and a pinch of salt, one teaspoon of ground cardamon seed and enough flour to make a dough as stiff as pie dough. Roll out thin and cut in diamond shapes three inches wide with a cut in the upper corner. Pull the point near the cut through the cut so it comes near the middle. Fry in lard like doughnuts. Place on paper to absorb the lard and sprinkle with powdered sugar.

MRS. O. OFFERDAHL.

Fattigman Cookies.

Yolks of six eggs and two whole eggs, one-half pound of sugar, two tablespoons of ground cardamon seed. Enough flour to make a dough as stiff as for pie crust. Roll out thin and cut in diamond shapes with a cut one inch long in the upper corner. Pull the point through the cut so it curves near the cut. Fry in hot lard.

MRS. O. OFFERDAHL.

Sand Bakkelse—Sand Cookies.

One and one-half cups of sugar, one and one-half cups butter and lard in equal proportion, one egg, two tablespoons of warm water, three cups of flour. Mix well together; take a lump of the dough as big as a walnut, cover the inside of patty tins and bake a light brown.

Ginger Cookies.

Two eggs, one cup sugar, one cup black molasses, one-half teaspoon salt, teaspoon ginger and cinnamon, four tablespoons boiling water. One teaspoon soda, flour enough to make them roll out nicely.

MRS. JENNIE SHAFER, Avon.

Rice Cakes.

One egg, beaten thoroughly into two cups of ordinary cooked rice, one tablespoon of flour; season with salt and one dash of cayenne.

Have liberal supply of oil in frying pan and when boiling hot drop from spoon into this and fry quickly.

MRS. KYLE.

Cheese Rice.

Two-thirds cup rice, washed and boiled. When thoroughly done turn into mixing bowl, add one beaten egg, one-half cup milk, tablespoon butter, one-fourth pound grated cheese, season with salt, cayenne pepper and parsley.

If desired, add two-thirds cup chopped walnuts; mix well, turn into baking dish, bake in moderate oven three-quarters of an hour.

JOSEPHINE E. WARDALL.

Rice Cakes.

One cup well-cooked rice, two eggs well beaten into this, one teaspoon sugar, salt and pepper to taste. Fry in hot oil or butter.

This can be seasoned highly with cayenne and curry if desired.

Rice Croquettes.

One-half cup rice boiled in one pint water and one pint milk. While boiling add lump of butter, two teaspoons sugar, three eggs, juice and grated rind of one lemon. Mix well, make into rolls a finger long, and dip first into yolk of egg, then in cracker crumbs and fry in hot oil.

PRACTICAL VEGETARIAN COOK BOOK.

Fruit Cake.

One pound English currants, one pound seeded raisins, one pound dates, one pound figs, one pound Graham flour, one-half pound candied citron, one pound English walnuts. Mince all separately, then mix all together, adding spice to suit the taste. It requires more spice than if the cake was cooked.

Put in a paper lined pan with a weight of fifty pounds on top to press, and let press for forty-eight hours. Keeps well.

VIRGINIA M. ELDER.

Golden Dressing.

One cup lemon juice, one cup pineapple juice, one and one-third cup sugar, eight eggs: mix all together and cook (stirring all the time) in double boiler until smooth, and let cool.

Black Pudding.

One quart of bread crumbs slightly moistened with cold water. One cup flour, one cup raisins, one cup currants, one cup molasses (New Orleans), one egg, butter the size of an egg, salt, vanilla, lemon, cloves, cinnamon and allspice, of each one-half teaspoon.

Mix dry ingredients, then into the molasses stir one rounded teaspoon of soda dissolved in a tablespoon of vinegar; stir all together and steam two hours. Serve with hard sauce.

VIRGINIA M. ELDER, Kirkland.

Fruit Mince for Pies.

Three bowls of chopped apples, one bowl raisins, one bowl currants, one-half pound sliced citron, one bowl brown sugar, one bowl molasses, one bowl cider, one bowl vinegar, two tablespoons each of cinnamon, cloves and nutmeg, one tablespoon each of salt and pepper, the grated rind and juice of three lemons. Just bring the mass to a boil, put in fruit while hot. Will keep a year.

E. J. CORNWELL, Kirkland.

Menus

"So far from woman's ambition leading her to attempt to act the man, she needs all the encouragement she can receive by the removal of obstacles from her path, in order that she may become the true woman."—
LUCRETIA MOTT.

A Christmas Dinner.

Table Decorations: Scarlet Carnations and Holly.
Eastern Oysters on the Half Shell.
Clear Soup, served with grated Parmesan Cheese Bread Sticks.
Boiled Halibut.   Hollandaise Sauce.
Cucumbers.
Timbales Regance.   Mushroom Sauce.
Roman Punch.
Turkey, stuffed with Chestnuts.
Cranberry Sauce.   Browned Sweet Potatoes.
French Peas.
Broiled Teal Duck on Toast,
with Hearts of Lettuce, French Dressing.
English Plum Pudding, Foaming Sauce.
Ice Cream with Maple Syrup and Chopped Nuts.
Sauce.   Fancy Cakes.
Glace Fruits.   Bonbons.
Black Coffee.   Cigars.
Coffee for ladies served in drawing room.

MRS. J. C. HAINES, Seattle.

A Washington State Dinner.

Table Decorations: Cactus Dahlias.
Olympia Oyster Cocktail.
Cream Yakima Tomato Soup.
Horse Heaven Bread Sticks.
Docewallops Rainbow Trout.
Shoe String White Rose Potatoes.
Vashon Island Broiled Quail on Toast.
Duwamish Valley Celery.
Jefferson County Venison, with Klickitat Chestnut Dressing.

Puyallup Cauliflower, with Drawn Butter Sauce.
Palouse Sweet Potatoes.   Kennewick Currant Jelly.
Spokane Whole Wheat Bread.
Snohomish Blackberry Pie, with Whipped Cream.
Wapato Watermelon.
Clark County Nuts.   Wenatchee Apples.
Tacoma Cigars.   Seattle Black Coffee.

MARGARET W. BAYNE,
NELLE MITCHELL FICK.

Menu for an Informal Summer Luncheon.

Cantaloupe.
Green Corn Soup.
Fried Chicken.
French Peas.   New Potatoes Creamed.
Pear Salad, Mayonaise Dressing.
Pineapple Float, Whipped Cream.
Lady Fingers.   Coffee.

MRS. ISAAC H. JENNINGS.

Cantaloupe.

The cantaloupe may be served in halves, filled with ice, or in halves filled with cherries, bananas and orange sweetened to taste, pouring teaspoonful of ginger ale over filling in each half.

Green Corn Soup.

(Pass salted wafers.)

One pint grated green corn, one quart milk, one pint hot water, heaping teaspoon of flour, two tablespoons of butter, one slice of onion.

Cook the corn in the water thirty minutes, mash with a potato masher. Let the milk and onion come to a boil; press the corn through a close seive, add to the milk (after removing the onion), season with butter, pepper and salt. Just before serving thicken with flour and serve in bouillon cups.

Escalloped Halibut.

(Pass olive sandwiches.)

Two cups cold boiled halibut, one-half cup fine bread crumbs, one teaspoon onion juice, one and one-half teaspoons finely chopped parsley, one and one-fourth cups milk, one large tablespoon butter, one cup white sauce, salt, cayenne.

Flake the halibut, removing all bone and skin; mix the fish with a white sauce made of one cup milk, one tablespoon butter, one-half teaspoon of salt, one-half teaspoon pepper thickened with flour, with this mix one tablespoon of parsley, the onion juice, salt and cayenne.

Butter the ramakins, put in the fish, smooth the top, cover with the remainder of the sauce, sprinkle with parsley, bread crumbs and bits of butter. Put the ramakins in a pan of boiling water for twenty minutes. Brown well on top.

Fried Spring Chicken.

Clean and wash well, and with a sharp knife cut open in the back. Dredge with pepper, flour and salt. Put equal quantities of butter and lard in hot frying pan. Then put in the chicken and keep it well covered until brown on both sides.

Cream Sauce for Chicken.

One pint of cream or milk, in which one spoonful of flour has been smoothly mixed. Take out the chicken and put the pan over the fire. Stir in the milk and flour. This makes good cream gravy.

Pear Salad.
(Pass Cheese Straws.)

Pare and halve Bartlett pears, removing the cores. Place half pear on lettuce leaf, putting a full teaspoon of mayonaise on top.

Mayonaise Dressing for the Above.

Yolk one egg, juice of one lemon, pinch of salt, and all the oil you care to use. Beat the yolk of the egg and drop oil until it begins to thicken. When very stiff add lemon juice alternately with oil until you have the quantity desired; salt to taste.

The secret of quick and easy making of mayonaise is to have all the ingredients ice cold.

Pineapple Float.

One cup grated pineapple, one cup pulverized or granulated sugar, white of one egg. Beat together until very stiff. Put on ice about a half an hour; when time to serve put in sherbet glasses with whipped cream on top, grating macaroons over all.

Lady Fingers.

Four eggs, one-half cup powdered sugar, one scant cup pastry flour, one teaspoonful vanilla. Beat yolks and whites separately very stiff. Sift in gradually the white sugar into the yolks of eggs, then add whites. Fold in the flour last. This recipe makes about thirty. Put two teaspoonfuls in each pan (lady finger pans), cook ten or twelve minutes.

MRS. ISAAC H. JENNINGS,
112 Queen Anne Avenue, Seattle.

Menu for an Informal Winter Luncheon.

Oyster Cocktail.
Celery Soup, with Croutons.
Broiled Veal Cutlets.
Creamed Carrots.   French Fried Potatoes.
Pineapple Salad, Mayonnaise Dressing.
Raisin Puffs, Fruit Sauce.

Coffee.   Nuts.   Candied Ginger.

MRS. ISAAC H. JENNINGS,
112 Queen Anne Avenue, Seattle.

Oyster Cocktail.

(Serve in cocktail glasses.)

To every glass three-fourths full of oysters allow one teaspoon of lemon juice, one tablespoon of strained tomato, two tablespoonfuls of tomato catsup, one-fourth teaspoonful Worcestershire sauce, one drop tobasco sauce, a little salt. If the tomato catsup is very mild put in no strained tomato and proportionately more catsup.

Celery Soup.

One bunch of celery, one pint of milk, one large tablespoon of flour, one pint boiling water, one large slice of onion, one cup whipped cream, pepper and salt and a small bit of mace. Cut the celery fine and boil in the water forty-five minutes. Let the milk with mace come to a boil, then skim these out and strain the celery into the milk. Cook eight minutes. Salt and pepper to taste. Pour into the tureen and just before serving stir in the whipped cream. An egg may be substituted for the cream.

Croutons for the Above.

Cut slices of bread into squares, lay in a pan, drip melted butter over them, place in the oven and toast until a light brown. Use as desired for garnishing or for serving with soup.

Cream Chicken.

(Pass green pepper sandwiches.)

One four and a half pound chicken, one can of mushrooms, four sweetbreads, one quart of cream, four tablespoonfuls of butter, five tablespoonfuls of flour or crackers. Boil the chicken and sweetbreads and when cold cut up as a salad. Put the cream in a saucepan with the butter; add the flour or cracker crumbs, stir until well melted and put the hot cream over, stirring all the time until it thickens; season highly with black and red pepper. Put in ramakins, covering the top of each with bread crumbs and pieces of butter. Bake twenty minutes.

Broiled Veal Cutlets.

Trim evenly, sprinkle salt and pepper on both sides; dip in melted butter and place upon the broiler; baste while broiling with melted butter, turning over three or four times. Serve with melted butter sauce or tomato sauce.

Creamed Carrots.

Scrape and wash six medium-sized carrots, quarter them and boil in salt water until soft; drain and mash; season with salt, pepper and butter the size of a walnut. Add a cup of rich cream and serve.

French Fried Potatoes.

Pare the potatoes and cut into three-cornered pieces. Fry as doughnuts in boiling lard. When brown add pepper and salt.

Pineapple Salad.

Take one can of sliced pineapple, place one sliced circle on lettuce leaf shredded; serve with spoonful of mayonnaise dressing.

Raisin Puffs.

Two eggs, two tablespoonfuls of sugar, one cup seeded

raisins, chopped fine and floured, one-third cup butter, two cups flour, three teaspoonfuls of baking powder. Steam in cups one hour and serve with fruit sauce.

Fruit Sauce.

One cup sugar, whites of one egg, one-half cup butter, one cup fruit juice. Cream the butter and sugar, stir in the white of egg beaten light, and lastly the fruit juice.

MRS. ISAAC H. JENNINGS.

Philadelphia Ice Cream.

One quart thick cream, two cups sugar, flavoring. Dissolve the sugar thoroughly in the cream and put into a gallon freezer, then fill the freezer to about three inches of the top with good sweet milk. If the cream is thick this will make very rich ice cream.

Some scald the cream, but this is not necessary, although many claim that the ice cream is finer by so doing.

Neapolitan Ice Cream.

One pint thick cream, four eggs, two cups sugar, flavoring. Dissolve sugar in cream, beat eggs, whites and yolks separately, until very light, put all together and add enough milk to fill freezer nearly full.

Strawberry and Pineapple Ice Cream.

To a quart of good cream just beginning to freeze add three-quarters of a cup of chopped pineapple and three-quarters of a cup of crushed strawberries, each of which have had a scant half cup of sugar sprinkled over two hours previously. Continue to turn the crank until stiff and serve within half an hour.

Pineapple Ice Cream.

Allow one quart of cream to one large pineapple. Pare the pineapple and chop it fine. Cover with sugar and allow it to stand three hours. Then press through a sieve, stir into the cream and beat, then pour into the freezer and freeze.

MISS MAY GRINNELL.

Sherbets.

A good sherbet foundation is one quart of water, one pint of sugar, one tablespoon of gelatine and the whites of three eggs. Soak the gelatine in a part of the cold water. Heat the rest of the water and the sugar together and add the soaked gelatine. When cold add the well-beaten whites of the eggs and beat thoroughly.

Lemon Sherbet.

Add the juice of six lemons to the above after it is cold. Then freeze.

Orange Sherbet.

Add juice of five sweet oranges and one large lemon to sherbet foundation.

Pineapple Sherbet.

One can of grated pineapple and the juice of one lemon. Add sherbet foundation and freeze.

A Good Fruit Ice.

One and one-half cupfuls of raspberries, three cupfuls of currants, one and one-third cupfuls of sugar.

MISS MARTHA JENNINGS, La Conner.

Combination Sherbet.

(Pineapple and lemon.)

One pint of canned pineapple, add one pint of water, juice of one lemon. Soak one tablespoon gelatine in one-quarter cup cold water. Cook one and one-half cups sugar and one-half cup water together for five minutes, then pour over gelatine and strain the mixture, but not the pineapple. Add a pinch of salt and let cool. Mix with it the lemon. Part one: Tablespoon of gelatine dissolved in one-quarter cup cold water, then add one-quarter cup hot water. Roll lemons (six if small, four if large), three cups of cold water and two cups sugar. Stir well.

MRS. C. W. CROPP, Tacoma.

Pineapple Sherbet.

Five cups water, grated rind of one lemon, two cups sugar, grated rind of one orange. Boil twenty minutes and let cool. One can grated pineapple, three oranges, two lemons, one tablespoon Knox's gelatine dissolved in one-half cup cold water. When the boiled sugar is cool, add gelatine and the fruit juice. Freeze in the usual way. The unbeaten white of one egg will give a little more body, but is not really necessary.

MRS. GEO. W. ALVERSON, La Conner.

Canning, Preserves, Pickles, Etc.

"Failure is impossible."—SUSAN B. ANTHONY.

This department was edited by Miss Martha Jennings and the unsigned recipes contributed by her.

The model housekeeper has always been noted for the wisdom and thrift she has shown in storing sweets for the winter.

The first essential to success with canning is that the fruit be in good condition; over-ripe fruit will yield poor results. Indeed, it is poor economy to can fruit when it has reached the stage where it must be attended to, at once, to be saved.

Then have good porcelain preserving kettles and time to attend simply to the matter at hand.

A good canning syrup is made after the following proportions: One pint of water and two coffee cups of sugar. Boil to a clear syrup.

Canned Peaches.

Pare and halve good, firm peaches and drop them into a clear boiling syrup made by boiling a coffee cup of sugar and a cup of water. This will make enough syrup for a quart of peaches when cooked. Boil until tender.

Canned Strawberries.

Hull the berries and measure them, then add to them as much sugar as berries, let stand over night and in the morning heat in the juice that the sugar has drawn from them. Put in glass jars and keep in dark closet so that the berries will keep their color.

Strawberries are especially fine canned in this way.

In canning I allow a cup of sugar to a quart of fruit, for most fruits and berries; sweet fruit, like pears, allow only half a cup, unless you wish them very sweet.

Baked Prunes.

Take ripe prunes, wipe clean but do not wash, put in dry

pan and to one quart of prunes add one cup of sugar; set in the oven and bake until tender. Be careful not to have the dish too full or your juice will run over.

Baked Pears.

To have baked pears perfect the pears must not be over-ripe. Three quarts of pears, measured after they are pared, two coffee cups of sugar, put them in a deep porcelain pan and completely cover with water, add more water if necessary, as the pears should be nearly covered with rich syrup when cooked. Bake about twelve hours, or until the pears are a rich, reddish brown. Serve with cream. They may be canned after baking and during the year make a delightful change from the usual canned pears.

Baked Apples.

Select apples of a uniform size and remove the core with a coring knife, fill the hole with sugar and a little cinnamon, and bake slowly, so that the apples may keep their shape. See to it that there is enough water added while the apples are baking so that there will be a nice syrup for them when cooked.

Baked Apples, No. 2.

Pare "Bell Flower" apples and cut in halves, remove cores and place in the pan so that the hollow where the core has been will be up; fill with sugar, a little cinnamon and a bit of butter. Bake slowly and serve warm with cream.

MRS. ROSE DUNLAP FLAGG.

Jellies.

In the making of jellies much depends on the fruit used; perhaps currant "jell" is easier than any other fruit, unless it be green apples. By mixing green apple juice with berry juices, such as blackberries, the flavor of the berry is not changed, and the "jelling" process is much quicker. Another happy combination is currants and raspberries.

In making black currant jelly, I think it is always better if half apple juice or red currant is used with the black currant. Rhubarb jelly is easily made if one-half apple juice is used. Cover the top of the jelly glasses with melted paraffine.

Currant Jelly.

Pick over and wash but do not stem the currants, press the juice from the raw fruit—there are fruit presses now that make this process very easy—measure the juice and put to boil; at the same time have an equal amount of sugar heating. When the sugar is warmed but not melted and the juice has boiled fifteen minutes, stir the sugar into the juice and boil five minutes more. Often it will not be necessary to boil the last five minutes, as it will "jell" as soon as the sugar is dissolved. This is a most reliable recipe.

Apple Jelly.

Quarter but do not pare the apples, fill a preserving kettle and cover them with cold water. Cook until the apple may be easily pierced with a broom straw. Put into a jelly bag and hang the bag so that its contents may drain all night. Do not press the contents of the bag. Use the same formula as in making currant jelly, excepting that if a sour jelly is desired less than one-half sugar may be used.

Housekeepers sometimes wonder why their jellies ferment as spring comes on. This is because the jelly has not been boiled long enough after the sugar is put in. Jelly may be cooked enough to "jell" perfectly and yet not keep a long time. Try longer boiling for the jelly that you expect to keep for months.

Crab Apple Jelly.

Remove stems and blossoms from fruit, wash well and stew half an hour in granite sauce pan (use enough water to cover the apples). Place fruit in a cheese cloth bag and let drain over night. Boil juice twenty minutes. Measure and add as many cups of heated granulated sugar as you have juice. Cook until thick. One or two rose geranium leaves added to juice at the same time sugar is added improves the flavor of the jelly. Put in jelly cups first rolled in cold water. When cold cover with melted paraffine and set in dark closet.

MRS. H. M. CHITTENDEN, Seattle.

Currants in Jell.

Stem half of the currants, heat them without sugar, press and strain the juice out of the remaining half, add the hot juice to the cold, measure and add a cup of sugar for each cup of juice.

Boil until it jells like ordinary currant jelly and drop the cooked currants into it.

This is fine with meats.

Fruit Juice.

Take any ripe fruit, pick over and wash, put in a porcelain kettle and cook half an hour or longer, according to the fruit; put in a bag and strain, return to kettle and add sugar or not as desired, heat very hot and put into air-tight jars.

This is fine as a foundation for punches, sherbets and many fancy desserts. Grape, strawberry, raspberry and blackberry are fruits that are especially fine for this purpose.

MRS. HELEN GRINDALL.

Canned Raspberries.

Pick the raspberries into a quart jar. Then boil one and one-half cups of sugar with a cup of water until it hairs. Pour this over the berries; screw on the top and set in boiling water over night.

MRS. I. E. SHRUGAR, Mt. Vernon.

Rhubarb Marmalade, Scotch Recipe.

Cut rhubarb fine and put pound of sugar to pound of fruit; let stand for two nights, then pour off syrup and cook until it thickens, then add the rhubarb and figs, one pound of figs to seven pounds of rhubarb. Add green ginger if desired.

MRS. G. HENSLER, Anacortes.

Orange Marmalade.

Slice thin seven oranges, measure and add as much cold water as oranges. Set away twenty-four hours; pour off the water, add fresh water, the same quantity as at first. Boil until tender; set away again for twenty-four hours, then add one and one-half times as much sugar as oranges and juice; boil until it jells.

MRS. O. W. HARDIN, San Diego.

Orange Marmalade, No. 2.

Grate the rind of oranges, cut the oranges in thin slices, take out seeds. To every pound of cut fruit add three pints of cold water, then boil until the oranges are tender—about two hours. Then weigh it and add to each pound of boiled fruit one and one-fourth pounds of sugar. Boil the whole till the syrup jells and the orange chips are quite transparent. This takes from twenty to forty minutes. Four oranges sliced make one pound.

MRS. D. R. TOMLIN, Kirkland.

Spiced Cherries.

The Royal Anne is the cherry that gives the best results in spicing. Put the cherries into a stone jar or porcelain pan. Heat one quart of good cider vinegar with two coffee cups of sugar; put into a muslin bag one teaspoon each of various spices, heat with the vinegar and sugar to the boiling point, then pour over the cherries and let stand over night. Repeat this a second time. Then put the cherries in glass bottles or jars, heat the vinegar a third time, pour over and seal. Fine with meats. Prunes are good spiced by this recipe, but the skins of the prunes must be pricked with a fork to prevent bursting.

Chow-Chow.

One-half bushel green tomatoes, one dozen green peppers (large sweet peppers), one dozen onions, chop all together. Stir in one pint of salt and let stand over night. Then drain, cover with vinegar and cook slowly one hour, then drain. Add three pints of sugar, two tablespoons of cinnamon, one tablespoon each of cloves, allspice, pepper and celery seed. One-half cup of white mustard seed, one pint of grated horseradish. Mix all together and add vinegar until thin.

MRS. C. E. FERGUSON, Columbia City.

Tomato Catsup.

One gallon tomatoes, or four cans, one cup vinegar, four teaspoons salt, four tablespoons sugar, one teaspoon each of allspice, cinnamon and nutmeg, one tablespoon mustard, one-half teaspoon cayenne. Cook slowly until the consistency of the usual bought catsup. The canned tomatoes are excellent for this purpose.

MISS MARTHA JENNINGS, La Conner.

Oil Pickles.

One hundred small cucumbers, peal, slice as for the table, sprinkle well with salt and let stand three hours; rinse and drain, then mix in two quarts of white onions that have stood in cold water three hours. Add, mixing thoroughly, one quart of best olive oil, three ounces white pepper, three ounces white mustard seed and one ounce of celery seed. Cover with white vinegar and can cold in air-tight jars. Do not forget to stir in a tablespoon of powdered alum, dissolved in hot water, to keep cucumbers firm and crisp.

MRS. A. K. GLASS, Seattle.

Mustard Pickles.

Two medium-sized cucumbers, one quart small onions, two cauliflowers, six green peppers (take out seeds), two quarts green tomatoes, cover with salt over night and add water to cover. In the morning scald the pickles in the liquid in which they stood all night.

Dressing: Two quarts vinegar, two cups brown sugar, one-fourth pound mustard, one-half ounce tumeric powder, three-fourths cup flour, two teaspoons celery seed. Pour over pickles hot and put in glass jars.

Variety Pickles.

One gallon of cabbage finely chopped, half gallon green tomatoes, one quart onions, all chopped fine; four tablespoons mustard, two tablespoons ginger, one tablespoon tumeric, one ounce celery seed, two pounds sugar, a little salt, one-half gallon good vinegar. Mix well and boil thirty minutes, then seal.

MRS. FRANK CURTIS.

German Mustard.

Slice two onions into a pint of hot vinegar, then let steep twenty-four hours. Bring to a boil, strain, pour while hot upon one-half pound of ground mustard and three tablespoons of sugar, beat well for five minutes, then add a tablespoon of olive oil, stir again for five minutes, set away to cool, then beat again if too thick. Add vinegar; put in airtight jars and keep in a cool place.

E. J. CORNWELL, Kirkland.

Chile Sauce.

Four large green tomatoes, four onions, four red or green peppers, chop together, drain off most of the juice and add four cups vinegar, three tablespoons of sugar, two of salt, two teaspoons each of cloves, cinnamon, ginger, allspice, nutmeg. Boil one hour and bottle for use.
MAUDE CHAMBERLAIN, Olympia.

Piccalilli.

Four quarts green tomatoes, four quarts cabbage, one quart onions, chop and salt over night, drain off juice in morning, two cups brown sugar, one cup white sugar, more may be added if desired; five cents' worth each of white mustard seed, celery seed and termice seed. Tie mustard and celery seed in muslin bags; cover well with cider vinegar, boil until tender. Remove seeds when ready to bottle.
MARY E. WALTERMIRE.

Green Tomato Pickles.

Slice one peck green tomatoes into a jar and sprinkle a little salt over each layer; let stand twenty-four hours. Drain off the liquid, place in a kettle, cover with a mixture of water and vinegar of equal parts and let simmer on the back of the stove until the tomatoes are tender, not soft; then drain off again and pour over the tomatoes this dressing: Take enough vinegar to cover the tomatoes, boil in it six teaspoons mixed spices tied in a cheesecloth bag, one teaspoon grated horseradish, three onions, cup sugar. It is a good plan to can the pickles hot, the same as canned fruit.
MRS. W. J. CROFT, Avon.

Beet Pickle Chow-Chow.

One quart cooked beets chopped fine; one quart raw cabbage choped fine; one cup grated horseradish, one teaspoon black pepper, one-quarter teaspoon red pepper, one tablespoon salt, two cups sugar. Mix well and cover with vinegar.
MRS. C. H. PURINGTON, Tacoma.

Nutmeg Melon Pickles.

Pare about fifteen melons for this amount of filling: Twelve peaches peeled and cut fine, one pint cherries canned, one-fourth cup each of candied orange peel and preserved ginger root. Cut fine and mix with the following: One

teaspoon ground cinnamon, one-half teaspoon coriander seed, one-half teaspoon mace or nutmeg. Fill the melon with this mixture after removing one natural section and seeds. Then sew section in with twine or tie in cheesecloth squares; boil until tender in the following syrup: One quart cider vinegar, three pounds sugar, one-half cup mixed pickling spices tied in bags. Set aside in stone jar. Boil for three mornings and pour over the melons while hot.
MRS. F. W. COTTERILL, Seattle.

Quick Pickles.

Cook green vegetables, such as string beans or cauliflower, ten minutes; drain and pour over them hot spiced vinegar, well seasoned with salt and pepper. Let stand twenty-four hours and they are ready for use.

Sweet Pickled Peaches.

Pare twenty pounds of cling peaches, layer them in a stone jar with sugar between. With this amount of peaches it will take about five cups of sugar to extract the juice.

To make syrup for pickles take ten pounds of sugar, two ounces of cinnamon and one and one-half ounces cloves; tie the spices in a thin cloth and drop in the syrup; put in the peaches, boil all together until the peaches are clear. Put away in stone or glass jars. Never add the first syrup which is extracted from the peaches. In this way less cooking is required and the peaches will be clearer and less shriveled.
MRS. M. J. WESSELS, Spokane.

Spiced Jelly.

To one gallon crabapple juice add one gallon sugar, one-half pint vinegar; into these ingredients drop one-half ounce whole cloves and one-half ounce stock cinnamon, enclosed in thin muslin bag. Boil all to jelly; put in glasses to cool.
MAY ARKWRIGHT HUTTON,
President Woman Suffrage Club, Spokane.

Mint Jelly.

Take two double handfuls of mint leaves, boil in a pint of water, strain into one gallon crabapple juice and add same amount of sugar as you have juice, then add a few drops of green fruit coloring and boil until it jellies. This is a delicious meat jelly. LaREINE BAKER,
Field Secretary East Washington Woman Suffrage Association, Spokane.

Confectionery

COMPILED BY JUNIOR EQUAL SUFFRAGE LEAGUE.

"I believe in woman's rights as much as in men's, and indeed, a little more."—THEODORE ROOSEVELT.

Nut Candy.

Measure one part white sugar, one part butter, four parts brown sugar, two parts chopped nuts or dates or a mixture of both, two parts water. Use coffee cup with two cups of brown sugar as basis, and above mixture makes one pie plate of candy.

Put the sugar and butter in a kettle and let it burn a little for flavor, after which add water and cook until a little on a spoon in cold water is as hard as your teeth and taste desire.

Butter the pie plate and surround it with cold water. A good plan is to put a cup or bowl in a dishpan full of water and set the pie plate on the bowl. This makes the candy cool evenly and prevents it from turning to sugar.

Put a layer of nuts on the bottom of the plate and then add more as the syrup is poured in order to mix them pretty well. This candy is more relished if let become perfectly cold than if eaten while warm.

Cocoanut Kisses.

Two cups of shredded cocoanut, one cup of powdered sugar. Mix well and add the well beaten whites of two eggs. Bake in rather hot oven until well browned.

HESTOR MILLER.

Cream Walnuts.

Take the white of one egg and mix in pulverized sugar until stiff; flavor, then take piece the size of a thimble, make into a ball and press a half of a walnut on each side of the ball. Roll in sugar.

PEARL G. SCHNEIDER.

Fudges.

Three cups of sugar, one cup of sweet milk, two squares of the best chocolate, boil eleven minutes; just before removing from the fire add a piece of butter as large as a walnut. Beat until it thickens and then pour into well buttered platter. A teaspoonful of vanilla flavoring may be added. Chopped nuts greatly improve this candy.

LUCY KANGLEY.

Sea Foam.

Three-fourts of a cup of "White Clover" syrup, three-fourths of a cup of water, two cups of sugar. Boil until it caramels when dropped in cold water, then remove from the fire and stir into it the stiffly beaten whites of two eggs; beat until it thickens and then pour into a well buttered pan. Nuts greatly improve this recipe.

EVA SHAW.

Caramels.

One cupful of grated chocolate, one cupful of white sugar, one-half cupful of West India molasses, one cupful of milk or cream; boil until thick, almost brittle, stirring constnatly. Turn it out onto buttered plates, and when it begins to harden, mark it into small squares so that it will break easily when cold. Some like it flavored with a teaspoonful of vanilla.

REINE DESILETS.

Nut Candy.

Two and one-half cups granulated sugar, one cup corn syrup, one-half cup hot water. Boil until it is brittle when dropped into cold water. Let cool a minute, then pour into the beaten whites of two eggs. Beat thoroughly and stir in any kind of nuts preferred, or mixed nuts, and vanilla to taste. Beat for several minutes and drop or spread on oiled paper and cut in squares.

MRS. JENNIE C. MEHAN, Roy, Wash.

White Taffy.

Three cups of sugar, half a cup of vinegar, half a cup of water, flavoring. Boil twenty minutes, cool and pull until white.

PEARL SCHNEIDER, Seattle.

Molasses Candy.

Over three scant cups of sugar pour one-quarter cup of water and dissolve slowly over the fire. Let boil about three minutes and add one cup of molasses, stirring all the time. As soon as it boils add another half cup of molasses. Stir constantly to keep from burning. Boil five minutes and add one cup of vinegar and vanilla to flavor. Cook until it hardens in cold water. Cool and cut in squares or pull.

PEARL SCHNEIDER, Seattle.

Marshmallows.

Two cups sugar, eight tablespoonfuls cold water. Set on slow fire until thoroughly dissolved, but do not let boil. To two tablespoonfuls of Knox's gelatine add six tablespoonfuls of warm water and let stand until entirely dissolved. (If this amount of water does not dissolve all the gelatine add a little more as the candy will not be good if any crystals remain.) Beat the dissolved gelatine into the syrup, getting it well blended. Return to the fire and heat to boiling point. Let partly cool and beat twenty minutes. Spread on platter and when set cut into squares and roll in powdered sugar. Good if rolled in dessicated cocoanut or dipped in melted chocolate.

BERNADINE DEVINE, Seattle.

Penouche.

Two cups brown sugar, one and one-half cups white sugar, one cup milk. Cook (with only enough stirring to prevent burning) until it forms a soft ball in water. Add butter size of walnut and pinch of salt. Take from the fire as soon as butter melts. Set to cool until you can put your hand on the bottom of the pan and find it just warm. (Do not cool it in a pan of water.) Beat until it sugars, then add one cup of chopped walnuts just before pouring into pan. Flavor with vanilla.

Seaform.

Four cups brown sugar, water enough to moisten all the sugar. Boil until it threads, then pour it slowly into two whites of eggs beaten stiff. Stir whites all the time you are pouring syrup. Add two cups chopped walnuts and vanilla to flavor. Beat until the mixture is stiff enough to hold its shape when a spoonful is dropped on paraphine paper. Drop by spoonfuls.

The same recipe may be used for fudge, using all white sugar instead of brown and adding two squares of chocolate to the sugar before cooking.

Turkish Delight.

One ounce sheet gelatine in half cup cold water. Let stand two hours or more. Do not put any more than a half cup to two full cups of granulated sugar. Add one-half cup cold water and dissolve a little over the fire, then add the soaked gelatine. Boil slowly twenty minutes. Have ready prepared the juice of one orange and one lemon. Stir this in the sugar when you take it off the fire; add a small amount of maraschino cherries cut in small pieces. Wet the pan you will put it in. It needs to be at least an inch thick in the bottom of the pan. Pour the candy in the pan and put the cherries around it afterwards. You can push them down in it more when it begins to congeal. Let it stand until next day. Cut in strips an inch wide. Roll in pulverized sugar. Cut in squares and roll all well in the sugar. Lay each one separately on dish, or paper is better, made the day before. Use it as it gets a little firmer.

It is very delicate. Of course the weather affects the gelatine and it will not be quite as firm in damp weather as in dry. Get the gelatine at the drug store.

Waugat.

Two cups granulated sugar, two-thirds cup glucose, one-half cup cold water. Cook until very brittle. Pour on one-third of syrup when syrup threads. Next third when syrup is done a trifle more; last third when syrup (tried in water) is hard and brittle. Pour on whites two eggs, beaten stiff, add cup nuts and vanilla. Beat until you can scarcely stir it. If it is right, it is dry.

Divinity.

Three cups granulated sugar, one cup syrup (either sea garden drips or golden drips), one cup cream, one pound walnut. Stir constantly. While cooling beat vigorously.

Fudge.

Two cups sugar, one cup milk, butter size of a walnut, one small tablespoon cocoa. Boil about fifteen minutes. When done pour into buttered plates and cut in squares. Chopped nuts and raisins may be added if desired.

MISS EVELYN JOHNSON, LaConner.

Fudge No. 2.

Take two squares of unsweetened chocolate or one teaspoon of unsweetened cocoa, two and one-half cups of sugar, one scant cup of milk, a piece of butter half as large as an egg; mix all together and cook over a hot fire for four minutes; beat all the time while cooking and continue to beat afterwards until smooth. Add vanilla while beating. Pour on a well-buttered plate and cut in squares.

EDNA GRAHAM, Avon.

Taffy.

One pint syrup—Tea Garden Drips won't do—one-half cup brown sugar, small piece butter; let boil slowly, stir often till it looks thick. Test by dropping a little in cold water; if it hardens it is done. Add one-sixth teaspoon soda, stir well, turn out on a buttered plate. As soon as cool enough butter your hands and pull the taffy; work it until it has a light yellow color. If flavoring is desired dip the fingers in the flavoring while pulling the taffy.

HATTIE STRUZENBERG, Avon.

Marshmellows.

Five cups sugar, three cups water, boil until it threads. Put one box Knox's gelatine in a bowl, use half of the lemon flavoring and the coloring tablet; dissolve with three tablespoons of water, pour the boiled sugar over it and beat one-half hour. Add vanilla. Put a paper on a platter dusted with cornstarch, pour contents in, let stand over night, then cut in squares.

MRS. EVELYNE OSBERG, LaConner.

Christmas Candy.

Put two cups of sugar (granulated or confectioner's), six tablespoonfuls of water and two tablespoonfuls of glucose in a pan; stir it up and boil until when you drop a bit in cold water you can take it up in your fingers and work. Pour in a platter and with a fork beat as you would an egg; it will get thick and white. Add any flavoring or nuts you like. Now take the fondant on a board and knead until smooth and creamy. Pinch off small pieces and shape them like chocolate creams, setting them on a board a few minutes before dipping. Have a small cake of chocolate and a piece of paraffne wax, about the size of a walnut, in a cup and set the cup in a basin of hot water until all is melted and very hot. Take a toothpick and stick into the lower side of the piece of fondant; dip quickly in the hot chocolate. By this process you will have as nice chocolate creams as you can get at any confectioner's.

The glucose may be purchased at a drug store or a confectioner's.

MRS. THOS. ROUSH, Mt. Vernon.

Peanut Candy.

Two cups sugar, one and one-half cups peanuts slightly chopped, one-fourth teaspoonful of salt. Melt the sugar; when melting stir in peanuts and pour in buttered plates.

MISS ANNA WHELAN.

Burnt Sugar Candy.

One cup of browned granulated sugar, one-half cup weak vinegar, cook until it hairs and set aside on the back of the stove; then melt one-half cup of white sugar and add to the above; then let come to a boil. Remove from fire and beat to a cream, adding nuts or cocoanut as desired. Spread on platter to cool. When cold cut in squares. Better when a few days old.

MRS. GERTRUDE MUSCOTT, Anacortes.

Butter Scotch.

Two cups light brown sugar, two of syrup, half cup butter; boil until it becomes brittle by dropping in water. Just as you take it off add quarter teaspoon bitter almond extract; pour on buttered plates and cut in squares when cold.

MRS. A. I. DUNLAP, LaConner.

Chocolate Caramels.

One cup sugar, half cup molasses, half cup milk, half spoon flour, butter size of walnut, quarter pound of chocolate; boil until hard; pour into a pan and mark in squares.

MRS. M. J. SULLIVAN, LaConner.

Stuffed Dates.

Seed the dates; insert a piece of walnut or a whole almond, press the date together again and roll in powdered sugar. This is a very dainty confection.

MRS. O. S. JONES, Walla Walla.

Vegetarian Department

One might fill a book with the many delicious dishes that can be prepared from vegetables and fruits. But the principle idea to be gained is that meals can be prepared quite as satisfactorily without the usual central flesh dish, with the vegetables only as accompaniments thereto.

The Editor will be very glad to answer any questions concerning vegetarian dishes, or give any information which twelve years experience as a vegetarian may have taught her.

SUBSTANTIAL DISHES FOR DINNER.

Nut Roast.

Two cups of ground walnuts, two cups ground breadcrumbs, two eggs well beaten, one-fourth pound butter, sage, pepper, onion and salt to taste. Pour boiling water over breadcrumbs until well moistened. Mix thoroughly all the ingredients. Bake one-half hour in a common bread pan. Turn out on platter and serve with tart jelly or cranberry sauce.

Nut Roast with Lentils.

Two cups ground walnuts, one cup ground breadcrumbs, one cup lentils cooked thoroughly, one cup stewed tomatoes, two eggs, season, add small onion, mix all together and bake one-half hour.

Rice Patties.

One cup of rice washed thoroughly; sprinkle into kettle of boiling water, with one-half teaspoon of salt. When kernels are tender pour into a colander and drain. When cold beat three eggs into the rice. Season with red pepper, salt and curry powder if liked. Fry in patties, in oil or butter. Serve with tart sauce.

Macaroni Escalloped.

Place macaroni in salted water, boiling hot, cook until tender and drain. Place in a baking dish alternately, a layer of macaroni and of grated cheese seasoning with red pepper and butter. Then pour over all enough milk to cover. Bake one-half hour in moderate oven.

Asparagus Shortcake.

Make a rich biscuit crust, roll out one-half inch thick and bake. Split, butter and fill with creamed asparagus. Serve. Peas may be used instead of asparagus.

Curried Rice and Tomatoes.

Put one can of tomatoes, or the equivalent in fresh tomatoes, into a granite kettle, add one small onion cut fine, wash thoroughly one-half cup rice and add to tomatoes. Cover tightly and cook very slowly on back of range. When rice is almost done season with butter, salt and curry powder. MRS. MILDRED KYLE.

Biscuit Pates.

Make rich baking powder biscuit, using rather large biscuit cutter. Have ready small mushrooms cut very fine and cooked in cream dressing well seasoned. Take a thin slice off bottom of biscuit, dig out center, put little pinch of butter in shell, fill with mushroom dressing and serve at once.

Bananas—Baked and Fried.

Peel the bananas, lay in baking dish, sprinkle with bits of butter and very little sugar, and bake. They cook very quickly. Bananas fried in butter are also very nice.

Delicious Fruit Mixture.

One pound figs, one pound dates, one pound prunes, one pound walnuts. Remove pits from dates and prunes, grind all together through Universal food chopper; add juice of two oranges; mix thoroughly; pack tightly in a mold. Slice thin when used.

MRS. MILDRED KYLE.

Beverages

*"Why women should vote*s *Because it is fair and right that those who must obey the laws should have a voice in making them."*—ALICE STONE BLACKWELL.

How to Make Good Coffee.

The old rule: One tablespoon of ground coffee for each cup of coffee and one for the pot is good. Put coffee into clean, scalded coffee pot and add as many cups of cold water as you have tablespoons of coffee, lacking one. Let come to a boil and boil one-half minutes; remove to back of stove and add half cup cold water, stirring well.

This will make absolutely clear coffee without other settling; the secret being the dash of cold water into the boiling liquid.

MISS MADGE JENNINGS, LaConner.

Good Tea.

First, the water must be freshly boiled; the teapot must be rinsed in hot water, so that its temperature may not lower the temperature of the water in which the tea is to steep.

Put in a teaspoon of tea for the first two cups and half a level teaspoon for each succeeding cup. Pour on the required amount of boiling water; set the teapot on the back of the stove or within the tea-cosy for about three minutes. Never on any account allow the tea to boil and never serve the first cup to a tea epicure.

MARGARET W. BAYNE, "Strathcluny," Kirkland.

How to Make Good Tea.

Heat two earthen teapots by pouring in boiling hot water and letting them stand. Bring fresh cold water quickly to boil in teakettle, and in its first minutes of boiling put the leaves in one of the teapots already hot; use about one-half teaspoon leaves to teacup of water; pour in the fresh boiling water and put on the cover quickly. Let stand three minutes and pour off the tea in the other hot teapot.

Tea strength is secured by briskly boiling water and tea quantity and not by long brewing. If tea is allowed to remain on the leaves longer than three minutes the only thing gained is tanin, which is, indeed, very injurious.

MRS. GEORGE B. SMITH, Anacortes.

A Cup of Excellent Chocolate.

Two squares Baker chocolate, two tablespoons sugar, pinch of salt, one teaspoon cornstarch, one and one-half pints milk. Grate chocolate and dissolve in two tablespoons boiling water. Add one cup of boiling water, the sugar, salt and cornstarch, dissolved. Boil five minutes. Add milk and serve with whipped cream. This makes eight cups.

MRS. IDA A. KEENE, Seattle.

Fruit Punch.

Juice of six lemons and six oranges, one can of pineapple minced, one quart strawberries crushed, three cups sugar, more if required, four quarts water and lime juice to taste. Serve with sliced banana or with cherries or in any way desired.

MRS. GEORGE E. VINCENT, Anacortes.

Fruit Punch.

Use two cups of fruit juice (strawberry, raspberry or any fruit desired) or mix several kinds with two cups of water, one-half cup of lemon juice, two cups of sugar; if the fruit used is sweet, use more lemon or add one-half cup of orange juice.

Apollonaris water is used in punches and is very nice. Some prepared fruit can also be added to give variety.

MRS. LOUSIA BERRY, Lexington Ky.

Fruit Eggnog.

One egg, white and yolk beaten separately; add to yolk any kind of desired fruit juice, orange, lemon diluted and sweetened, or other fruit either cooked or uncooked. Stir in white of egg last. A delightful drink.

MISS GERTRUDE WALLACE, Stanwood.

Mountaineers' Chapter
Cooking in Camp

"Woman must be enfranchised. She must be a slave or an equal; there is no middle ground."

This chapter will be found equally good for campers, prospectors, hunting parties and mountain climbers; indeed, the much space devoted to this chapter is due to the ever-growing practice of all classes to live out of doors during our long, delightful summers.

It also contains many recipes good all the year round.

How to Build a Camp Fire.

In building a camp fire quickly, the first essential is dry wood. A dead cedar limb, a dead standing tree commonly called a "snag," a windfall or the heart of a green tree will furnish good wood to kindle a fire.

Cut the wood fine and place in the form of a teepee with shavings inside and place larger wood over all; have a back log or two side logs so as to create a draft.

In case no dry wood is procurable or in rainy weather the following method will work where all others fail: Take a piece of candle an inch or two long (no one who has used it for this purpose will ever be out without a piece of candle in his pocket), and place it where the fire is wanted, then place shavings or fine wood, the finer the better, in the form of a tepee over the candle, adding larger wood to the outside and top of the teepee. Do not light the candle until a good lot of wood has been gathered. Have patience when building a fire in wet weather.

The principle of this method is that the candle dries and ignites the damp shavings and they in turn dry and ignite the larger wood.

It takes a little practice to build the teepee just right so that the wood will fall together while burning. This is the secret of keeping the fire going. The old saying is, "One stick will not burn, but two will."

Keep your fire together.

L. A. NELSON, 522 New York Block, Seattle.

Provisions for Four People One Week.

Flour, 18 pounds.
Cornmeal, 6 pounds.
Hardtack, 6 pounds.
Beans (army), 7 pounds.
Rice, 4 pounds.
Salt pork, 6 pounds, or substitute a small ham.
Bacon, 6 pounds.
Potatoes, 15 pounds.
Onions, 4 pounds.
Butter, 4 pounds.
Dried fruits, 4 pounds.
Oatmeal, 2 pounds.
Syrup, 1 quart.
Coffee, 2½ pounds.
Tea, ½ pound.
Sugar, 6 pounds.
Milk (evaporated), 7 cans.
Salt, 3 pounds.
Cornstarch, 1 pound.
Cheese, 1 pound.
Raisins, 1 pound.
Currants, 1 pound.
Sardines, 6 cans.
Candles, 6.
Pepper, ¼ pound.
Mustard, ¼ pound.
Baking powder, ½ pound.
Baking soda, ½ pound.
Soap, 1 bar laundry.
Matches, 1 large box.
Ginger, ⅛ pound.
Allspice, ⅛ pound.
Pickles, ½ gallon.
Vinegar, 1 pint.
Erbswurst, 1 pound.
Beef extract, ¼ pound.
Macaroni, 1 pound.
Dried beef, 2 pounds.
Sweet chocolate, 6 half-pounds.
Lemons, 2 dozen.

Prepared by Asahel Curtis, Chairman, 627 Colman building, Seattle, and L. A. Nelson, 522 New York block, Seattle, Outing Committee for "The Mountaineers."

List of Kitchen Outfit.

3 kettles (granite ware), 1 2-quart, 1 1-gallon, 1 1½-gallon, with loose wire handles for telescope packing.
1 frypan (long cold handle).
Reflector (for baking with open fire).
2 bread pans for reflector.
1 2-quart coffee pot.
1 2-quart tea pot.
1 3-gallon pail (enamel).
Rolling pin (vinegar bottle).
Potato masher (vinegar bottle).
Corkscrew.
1 can opener.
1 quart pitcher (for canned syrup and cream).
1 dishpan, 14 inch.
1 salt and pepper shaker (¼ pound can of pepper).
3 6-inch milk pans (for serving).
1 ladle, 1 gill.
2 large basting spoons.
1 butcher knife, 8-in. blade.
½ dozen each knives and forks.
½ dozen each spoons (two sizes).
½ dozen plates.

½ dozen cups (loose handle).
½ dozen bowls (for soup and cereals).
1 small collander.
1 pancake turner.

For permanent use, granite or enamel ware is the most desirable, as it can be cached. For a few days' or weeks' trip, when the outfit will be discarded at the end of the trip, or when space and weight in transportation must be considered, tinware will be found just the thing.

NELSON AND CARR.

MOUNTAINEERS' RECIPES FOR FOUR PERSONS.

Compiled and edited by a committee consisting of L. A. Nelson, 522 New York Block, Seattle; Dr. Cora Smith Eaton, 482 Arcade Building, Seattle; Robert Carr, Cooks' Union, Local 33, Seattle. (Carr was official chef for The Mountaineers, seasons of 1907 and 1908, on Mt. Olympus and Mt. Baker trips.)

Tea.

Into two quarts of fresh water, boiling hard, put a loose cheesecloth bag containing four heaping teaspoons of tea. Cover and let stand by the fire for five minutes, but do not boil. Then remove the bag of tea, as leaving it in will make the tea bitter. Or, if the bag is not convenient, pour the tea off the leaves after it has steeped five minutes.

EATON.

Coffee.

The coffee should be ground fine. To two quarts of cold water add eight dessert spoonfuls of coffee, place over fire and bring to a boil and let boil two minutes, then remove from fire and from the height of a foot add one-half cup cold water to clear coffee.

NELSON.

Cocoa.

Make a paste with eight tablespoonfuls of cocoa and a little cold water. Put into two quarts of boiling water and boil ten minuets. Sweeten and add condensed milk.

NELSON.

Baking Powder Bread.

To two pints of flour add two heaping teaspoonfuls of baking powder, one teaspoonful salt and bacon fat size of an egg. Mix thoroughly while dry. Now add cold water enough to make a smooth dough. It should be just thin enough to pour into bread pan, which must first be greased. Place in rack of reflector or baker before the fire and bake until a fork or stick inserted in the bread shows no dough when withdrawn.

Biscuit.

Same as above, except mix a little stiffer.

Corn Bread.

Same as bread except use one pint cornmeal and one pint flour, and add milk and sugar.

NELSON.

Carr's Yeast Bread.

Two potatoes should be peeled and sliced and cooked till soft. In the meantime, have a cake of "Magic Yeast" dissolving in a cup of lukewarm water. When the potatoes are soft so that you can squeeze them, put a cupful of flour into the boiling potato water, to scald it, and work it in to break up the lumps.

Let it cool to lukewarm. Add the yeast cake to the lukewarm mixture and set it in a warm place for twelve to fourteen hours, till it ferments. The yeast thus prepared will be used in the proportion of one cup of yeast to two cups of water. This yeast will keep for two weeks, in a cool place.

1 cup yeast.
1 tablespoonful salt.
1 tablespoonful lard.
2 cups warm water.
1 tablespoonful sugar.

Mix and work in enough flour to form a soft batter by throwing the dough over itself and patting it, to let air into it. Let stand one hour, and work up stiff, until it will take no more flour, so that if you squeeze the dough hard it will not stick to your hands.

Then let it rise to double its size, which will take probably six hours, then knead it into loaves. If not convenient to bake it at six hours, punch it down again in the pan, and let it rise again, which will improve it. In one to one and one-half hours it will be again ready for the oven.

Do not force rising bread by too much heat. Bake bread just an hour. Do not open the oven often, not at all for thirty minutes, if you want good color. After the bread is out of the oven rub water over the loaf, to give it a gloss and prevent it from cracking. If the yeast has fermented well, the bread will certainly rise.

CARR.

Macaroni with Cheese.

Boil macaroni in salted water about thirty-five minutes, till soft. Season with pepper and salt. Then add canned cream and diced cheese. Put into a greased pan and sprinkle cheese on top. See that there is enough liquid to cover the macaroni when you pat it down. Put it into a medium oven about twenty minutes to brown.

CARR.

Macaroni with Tomatoes.

With what is left over of the macaroni and cheese, mix canned tomatoes and work them in well. Cook twenty minutes in a medium oven or until brown. CARR.

Bannocks or Open-Fire Bread.

Into one quart of flour work one tablespoonful of bacon fat, two teaspoonfuls of baking powder and a pinch of salt. Mix with water or milk into a soft dough.

In the meantime have an open fire going steadily. Put a part of the dough into a well-floured skillet. Cook the under side slowly until a few small air holes appear on the top, then prop the pan with a stick edgewise before the fire and cook the upper side until brown, without disturbing the cake by turning it.

If an attempt is made to cook it on both sides in the pan over the fire, it will fall and the baking powder has been useless, for there will be a doughy streak in the middle which it will be impossible to cook.

CARR.

Griddle Cakes.

Some of the specially prepared "pancake flours" will

do, such as "Peacock's Buckwheat Flour." Mix with milk to a thin batter. Cook on a liberally greased griddle.

CARR.

Boiled Rice.

Thoroughly wash and rinse one cup of rice in cold water, drain and place in at least two quarts of boiling water in an uncovered pot and boil until done, adding water as it boils away. Do not stir it or it will burn. When done, add two teaspoonfuls salt.

NELSON.

Oatmeal Mush.

Two cupfuls of oatmeal, two teaspoonfuls salt to two quarts of boiling water. Let it cook thirty minutes.

CARR.

Cornmeal Mush.

Sprinkle with the hand a pint of yellow cornmeal into three pints of rapidly boiling salted water, stirring all the time. Cook for half an hour, stirring most of the time to prevent scorching. Fine, if set aside to cool and then sliced and fried and served with maple syrup. Should be mixed a little stiffer for frying.

CARR.

Boiled Beans.

Soak for twelve hours a pint of white beans. Pour off the water and add two quarts of fresh water. If the water is changed twice as soon as it comes to a boil, the bean flavor will be more delicate. Then add a small piece of salt pork or bacon cut up, one pint of tomatoes, a bay leaf, an onion and two teaspoonfuls of salt and boil until tender.

CARR.

Baked Beans.

Same as boiled beans except that when the skin will break easily put them into a dripping pan and add two tablespoonfuls of molasses, salt and white pepper and bake in a slow oven four hours or until tender. If you add half a cupful of canned tobatoes before putting into the oven it improves them.

CARR.

Bean Soup.

Wash two cups white beans and boil in about two quarts of water until, if placed on a spoon and blown upon, their skins will split or shrivel, or if squeezed they mush; drain, add half teaspoonful salt, a dash or two of pepper, salt pork or bacon cut fine. Boil until beans are cooked to pieces. This can be aided by stirring. As water boils away, add more to keep required quantity. Do not strain, as you lose food value by so doing. Do not add salt and other seasoning until after beans have become soft.

NELSON.

Or make stock from extract of beef, one ounce to two quarts water, and add one can of baked beans and stir well while heating to boiling point.

ANNA HUBERT.

Prospector's Soup.

Put two tablespoonfuls of bacon fat or butter and three tablespoonfuls of flour into a sauce pan and keep stirring over a medium fire until flour is golden brown. Work in, slowly at first, one quart of boiling water, stirring all the time, until smooth. Add one-half can of milk, salt and pepper to taste. If an onion or onion extract is added it will improve it.

CARR.

Erbswurst Soup.

Dissolve in cold water one-third of a package of erbswurst, to take out the lumps, add to two quarts of boiling water, flavor with onion and boil ten to fifteen minutes. Erbswurst is the celebrated "pea meal sausage," the German army ration, and is very nutritious. Season it just as it is ready to serve. A slice of lemon in each bowl served is good if obtainable.

CARR.

Rice Tomato Soup.

Into two quarts of boiling water put a handful of rice and a small onion diced, and cook for thirty minutes or till rice is soft. Then add one pint canned tomatoes and cook ten minutes longer, adding one ounce beef extract and one-half teaspoonful of salt and a little white pepper before serving.

CARR.

Pearl Barley Soup.

Into two quarts boiling water put one-fourth cupful of pearl barley and cook one and one-half to two hours till done. Flavor with onion and add any left-over cold meats diced. Just before serving put in one ounce beef extract and enough more hot water to make up for evaporation.

CARR.

Creamed Codfish and Potatoes.

Soak for twelve hours one cupful of shredded codfish. Drain off the salt water and add cold water and bring it to a boil and cook until soft. Drain. Have ready four cupfuls boiled potatoes quartered and two quartered stewed onions.

Prepare two pints of white sauce as below, without salt, and while it is boiling stir in the codfish and then put in the potatoes and onions.

CARR.

White Sauce.

Melt slowly a piece of butter the size of an egg and stir in thoroughly a heaping dessertspoonful of flour until perfectly smooth. Then add slowly one cupful hot milk and boil three minutes, stirring all the time. Season to taste before serving. This can be made into a sweet sauce for puddings by adding sugar and flavoring.

CARR.

To Cook Trout in the Forest.

First catch your trout.

Then with a sharp knife split lengthwise along the spine from the inside, cutting from the front while holding the fish on its back on a log, stump or piece of bark.

Salt and pepper plentifully the separated halves on their cut sides, allowing them to remain several hours or over night in a covered pan, when they may be well rolled in flour or cornmeal and dropped, salted side down, into a skillet of hot fat (bear's lard if obtainable), and fried over embers left from a fire of fir or hemlock bark, turning the pieces over after a short time. Do not cover the skillet.

Trout under one-half pound in weight may be similarly treated without splitting.

GRANT W. HUMES, Port Angeles, Wash.

To Fry Venison in Camp.

Place your meat on a flattened log or stump and cut the slices to medium thickness. Hack well with a knife to make them tender. Place in hot bacon fat and fry about two minutes without cover, then salt and pepper, turn and continue frying for three minutes. If you desire the meat well done fry another minute or two. This manner of cooking renders the meat more toothsome and at the same time retains the juices in the meat.

WILL E. HUMES, Port Angeles, Wash.

Venison Chops—Hunter's Style.

Fry the chops in the skillet with plenty of bacon grease, until, when you stick in a fork, the blood will not come out.

Take out the chops and pour off about half of the top of the grease. Put in one tablespoonful of flour for four chops and stir till quite smooth and a little brown. Then pour in one cup of hot water, working the mixture while pouring in the water. Season to taste with salt and pepper just before removing from the fire.

CARR.

Spanish Sauce for Meats.

Dice one large onion, one green pepper and one slice of ham. Put in a saucepan with a chunk of butter and fry them. When the onions are about half cooked put in one quart of tomatoes and stew about one hour.

CARR.

Roast Meat.

Prepare piece of meat, say six pounds, by removing surplus fat and tissue.

Place in skillet containing a little hot fat, and sear the roast on all sides to keep in the juices. Then sprinkle well with flour and salt and pepper and place in a pan in the baker or oven and cover bottom of pan with water. If the meat is a little strong or "gamey," a few slices of onion or a sprinkling of dried onion will enhance the flavor. Baste frequently with the gravy and turn when half done, basting as before.

CARR.

Bacon or Ham.

Bacon or ham can be sliced and either fried or broiled over a slow fire.

Boiled Ham.

A medium-sized ham should be put on to cook in cold water and boiled three and one-quarter hours, or until the small bone in the end is loosened. Then let the ham stand in the water it is boiled in until cold. CARR.

Chipped Beef in Cream.

Slice the dried beef as thin as possible. Fry it for a minute or two in a little hot fat, such as bacon grease or butter, then cover with hot water and simmer for ten minutes. Make a paste of two tablespoonfuls of flour in cold water and stir in to thicken the gravy. Add one-fourth can of milk before serving.

ALICE B. TAYLOR.

Overland Trout.

Make a stiff batter with one cup of flour, one pinch of salt and one-half teaspoonful of baking powder. Cut cold boiled or fried bacon into strips, dip in batter until well covered and fry in hot fat till brown. CARR.

Stewed Fruits.

Clean one pint evaporated fruit and put into two quarts of cold water. Simmer until nearly done, then add one-half cup of sugar and a little ground spice as you take it off the stove. Use cinnamon with apples, nutmeg with apricots and lemon and cinnamon with prunes. An iron or tin pot will discolor the fruit and spoil its flavor. CARR.

Carr's Hardtack Pudding.

(The Bread Pudding of the Forest.)

Take the broken scraps of hardtack and soak them over night. In the morning, sweeten with sugar and flavor with nutmeg and squeeze it well to break up all lumps.

1 lb. hardtack.   ¼ lb. almonds.
¼ lb. raisins.   ¼ lb. currants.

Mix and put into a buttered pan and pat it down level. Sprinkle sugar on top to make it tasty and put dabs of butter all over. Bake in a slow oven an hour and a quarter. Serve with the following sauce:

Melt slightly one-half cupful of butter, then work in quite smooth about two tablespoonfuls of flour or less, making it not too stiff. Then while cooking it, add slowly hot water and canned milk (one part of milk to two parts of water), stirring all the time. Boil three minutes. Flavor with lemon and sweeten well. The real lemon and rind diced up makes the best flavoring. CARR.

Carr's Fruit Cake.

A valuable ration for carrying the fruit and nuts desired on a hard climb:

Two teaspoonfuls baking powder sifted with one quart of flour, butter or bacon fat size of two eggs, one-half teaspoonful salt, one cup sugar, one level teaspoonful each of cinnamon, ginger and nutmeg, one cup currants, one-half pound raisins, one cup citron, one cup almonds.

Rub flour, baking powder, sugar, butter and spice between the hands well, then mix fruit and nuts. Make a good stiff mixture with diluted canned milk. Bake one and one-quarter hours in a medium oven.

Cornstarch Pudding.

Put on a quart of water to boil, well sweetened. Dissolve one-fifth of a pound package of cornstarch in cold water and gradually stir into the boiling sweetened water; then add one-half can of cream, a pat of butter and some extract of lemon or vanilla. Cook five minutes, then put into molds, or in a pan, and set away to cool. CARR.

Ginger Cake.

Take one quart of flour, one cupful of sugar, two teaspoonfuls of baking powder, one-half cupful of butter or lard, one teaspoonful of ginger, one pinch of salt and rub between the hands until all are well mixed. Put in one and one-half cupfuls of molasses or syrup and two cupfuls of warm milk or water. Stir well, put into a greased pan and bake in moderate oven for forty minutes. CARR.

Mince Meat.

Stew or steam two pounds dried apples for ten minutes, or till they are about as soft as fresh green apples; then chop them fine. Stew two pounds of raisins and two pounds of currants in plenty of water for thirty minutes. Chop or dice one pound citron and two pounds suet. Boil a piece of lean beef until tender, and when cold chop or run through sausage machine. Mix in with the fruit, sweeten well, then spice with one-quarter pound of cinnamon, two tablespoonfuls of allspice, two tablespoonfuls of nutmeg and two tablespoonfuls of ginger. . CARR.

"Dough Gods."

A mountaineer's list of recipes would not be complete without the ration to which the trail-maker or scout is reduced when the supplies are nearly exhausted and there is little left besides flour and salt. However, hard necessity may be the only guide followed at such a time.

To one quart of flour, two teaspoonfuls of baking powder and one teaspoonful of salt, add enough water to make a stiff dough. Mix like flapjacks and bake in a frying pan.

NELSON.

Men's List of Absolute Necessities—Man Pack Trip.

To Wear.

1 Suit woolen underwear.
1 Overshirt.
1 Pair socks.
1 Suit clothing.
1 Pair mountain boots.
1 Felt hat.
1 Handkerchief.
1 Extra pair drawers.

In Pack.

1 Sheath or pocket knife.
1 Matchbox (waterproof)
1 Pocket compass.
1 Neckerchief.
1 Woolen sweater (to be used in place of undershirt when washing undershirt.)

3 Pair socks.
1 Pair gloves.
1 Towel.
Soap.
Comb.
Toothbrush.
Adhesive tape.
Surgeon's bandage.
1 Sleeping bag.
1 5x7 "A" silk tent (for two persons).
Needle and thread.
Small carborundum stone.
Fishing tackle.

NELSON.

Men's Personal Outfit for One Month's Outing—Pack Horse Trip.

To Wear.

1 Suit clothing.
1 Suit woolen underwear.
1 Overshirt.
1 Pair socks.
1 Handkerchief.
1 Neckerchief.
1 Pair mountain boots.
1 Soft felt hat.
1 Pair suspenders or belt.
1 Sheath or pocket knife.
1 Waterproof match safe.
1 Pocket compass.
1 Pair gloves.
1 Watch.

Pack.
1 Extra pair pants.
1 Overshirt.

3 Pair socks.
1 Suit underwear.
1 Towel.
1 Handkerchief.
1 Pair tennis shoes.
1 Woolen sweater.
1 Sleeping bag, complete.
1 Canteen.
Boot grease.
1 5x7 "A" tent (for two persons).
1 2½-pound axe.
1 Dunnage bag to pack this outfit in.
1 Pack sack.
Toilet articles.

NELSON.

Women's List for the Mountains.

1. Sleeping bag, consisting of three bags, one inside the other.
    (1) Waterproof shell, of kahki or rubber or paraffined canvas or oiled silk.
    (2) Double wool blanket bag.
    (3) Comfort padded with wool bats, the comfort folded and sewed together as a bag.
2. Tramping suit:
    (1) Bloomers or knickerbockers.
    (2) Short skirt, knee length, discarded on the hard climbs.
    (3) Wool waist or jumper.
    (4) Sweater or heavy coat.
3. Three pairs of cotton hose.
4. Three pairs of boys' wool socks to wear as the second pair of hose to prevent chafing.
5. Mountain boots to the knee, with heavy soles, heavy enough for hob-nails, and these must be placed in soles before starting, using 3½ eighths Hungarian nails in the instep as well as in the heels and soles.

6. Lighter shoes, like tennis shoes, for camp.
7. Gaiters to wear with the light shoes.
8. Chamois heel protectors, worn next to the skin, or adhesive plaster, to prevent blistering the heel.
9. Two winter undersuits, ankle length and long sleeves.
10. Two lighter undersuits, ankle length and long sleeves.
11. One dark colored night robe or pajamas.
12. Hat, light weight, with medium brim.
13. Mosquito head net or bee veil.
14. Smoked goggles.
15. Heavy gauntlet gloves.
16. Three bandana handkerchiefs.
17. Rubber poncho, or slicker coat.
18. Toilet articles:
    (1) Soap.
    (2) One bath towel.
    (3) Wash cloth.
    (4) Cold cream.
    (5) Glycerine and rosewater.
    (6) One ounce 5 per cent salicylic acid in lanoline, a salve for blistered or tender feet.
    (7) Small piece of naptha laundry soap.
    (8) One 10c tin wash basin.
19. One stick actor's grease paint, any color, to prevent sunburn on the snow.
20. Canteen.
21. Drinking cup, preferably a tin cup with loose handle, to hang on the belt.
22. Alpenstock, a little higher than the head, the stick made of hickory if obtainable, the steel point well sharpened.
23. Candles, stearic wax candles the best.
24. Matches.
25. A strong jack knife.
26. Writing materials, wrapped in an oilcloth.
27. Needles and thread.
28. One gross assorted safety pins.
29. Clippings for the campfire entertainments.
30. Calks for snow and ice climbing, two sets, making 32 of No. 5 for soles and 16 of No. 7 for heels.
31. Gum to keep mouth and throat from getting dry in climbing.

32. Four muslin squares, or extra bandanas, for wrapping and tightly tying up various groups of articles.
33. 5x7 "A" silk tent, weight 3½ pounds, for two persons.
34. Wall bag, of canvas or kahki or denim or cretonne, 18x 36 inches, with several pockets, each pocket box-pleated and with a flap which ties down and closes pocket. This is the "mountain chiffonier."
35. One dunnage bag, 3 feet long and 18 inches wide, with canvas handles at bottom and sides. This bag will carry all that goes on the pack train.

Note—Taking out what she wears, this outfit should weigh about forty pounds. It can be cut down for a hard pack trip where the baggage limit is less. The list is prepared especially for trips including climbs on glaciers and snow fields. A few items, such as goggles, alpenstock, grease paint and heavy underwear could be omitted for the ordinary outing.

Any cotton undergarments worn will be more serviceable if made of colored gingham.

CORA SMITH EATON, M. D.

Sailors Recipes

"The ballot is an educator and women will become more practical and more wise in using it."

Furnished by Robert Carr, Cooks' Union, Local 33, Seattle. Mr. Carr has had about five years' experience as cook and steward on board sailing vessels, all over the world, and has had the record of being a most popular cook, one vessel delaying its date of sailing a week in order to get him.

Dolphin or Bonita.

Test for Poison: Dolphin are good to eat part of the year, and are poisonous at times. Boil a copper coin with the dolphin. If it tarnishes the copper, the dolphin is not fit to eat. If it remains bright, the dolphin is good.

To Make Fresh Water "Spin Out" When Supply Is Limited.

1. Catch and use all the rain water you can, in rain bags.
2. Boil potatoes in sea water.
3. Mix bread with sea water, as it improves the bread.
4. To soak salt meat or salt fish, put in a bag or rope bucket and hang over the stern of the ship for a while.

Sea Birds.

Almost all sea birds are good eating. To get rid of the fishy taste, skin them, for that is where the fishy taste is found. Stuff the birds with a sage dressing and lay a piece of salt pork all over each breast. Roast them and they are equal to any game.

Seal Livers and Seal Hearts.

Excellent, except when the seals are fasting during the breeding season.

Tail of a Shark.

Good eating. Boil it with plenty of spice and serve with a cream sauce.

Or cut it up in small pieces, lay it in a dish, season with salt and pepper and lay on whole spice. Cover with vinegar. Bake thirty minutes and set it aside to cool. Serve cold.

Porpoise.

Cut out the fillets of porpoise, which is all that is good. Soak in salt water to draw out the blood. Cut holes in it and insert pieces of fat pork. Braise it (sear it) in a very hot oven. Put it in a kettle with a can of tomatoes, one-half cupful of vinegar, one-half pound salt pork, brown crust of bread size of a whole cut of an ordinary loaf, and, if possible, add carrots and turnips and onions.

Simmer for two and one-half hours. Take out the meat and strain off the gravy and serve separately. If the gravy is too strong, weaken with water, leaving the carrots and turnips in the gravy.

List of Store Seasonings Sufficient for Twelve Months' Voyages.

12 Bunches of marjoram. 24 Bunches of parsley.
18 Bunches of thyme. 2 Pounds of cloves.
18 Bunches of sage. 1 Pound of mixed spice.
12 Bunches of mint. 1 Pound of bay leaves.

N. B.—As the supply of these articles is somewhat limited, it is recommended that the cook bring the stock up to the above list before sailing.

Pea Soup.

Ingredients.

8 Quarts water. 2 Tablespoonfuls dripping.
3 Pints spit peas. 4 Pound piece of half cooked
2 Carrots, or piece of turnip salt pork, or sufficient
  same size. salt stock to season.
2 Tablespoonfuls celery seed. 1 Teaspoonful sugar.
2 Tablespoonfuls flour. 6 Leaves of mint.

Method: Make the dripping hot in a large stew pan, slightly brown the flour, add celery seed and water, and stir well until boiling, then add the peas, mint, sugar and carrots, and simmer for two hours in covered pan. Add the pork, or stock,, and simmer another half hour. Rub all through a wire sieve and warm up again before serving. It is not advisable to steep peas all night in warm weather as the water becomes sour.

Soup and Bouilli.

Ingredients.

4 Quarts fresh stock.
4 Tablespoonfuls flour.
4 Tablespoonfuls dripping.
½ Bunch marjoram.
1 Small carrot.
2 Small onions.
1 Pound shin beef.
A pinch of cayenne.
Salt to taste.

Method: Make the dripping hot in a stew pan. Brown the beef cut small, take it out, brown the onions cut small, take these out and brown the flour a good color, add the stock gradually, keeping it well stirred. When simmering add the marjoram tied in a piece of muslin, and leave it in ten minutes. Then add the carrot cut small, season and simmer one hour. Before serving remove all fat.

Curried Salt Beef.

(Cold Meat Cookery.)

Ingredients.

1 Pound cooked salt beef.
2 Small potatoes.
2 Dessertspoonfuls of curry powder.
1 Dessertspoonful flour.
1 Tablespoonful butter or dripping.
1 Good sized onion.
1 Teaspoonful vinegar.
1 Pinch sugar.
½ Pint water.

Method: Make the dripping or butter hot in a stew pan. Brown the onion cut small, add the curry powder and flour dry and mix till smooth, then add the water gradually, and keep it well stirred. Have the meat and potato cut small. If the meat is too salt, scald it and make it fresh before adding it to the curry. Add the other ingredients and simmer slowly thirty minutes.

Hot Pot Tom Bowling.

Ingredients.

25 lbs. potatoes.
6 lbs. beef or preserved mutton.
3 lbs. onions.
½ lbs. dripping or lard.
½ oz. pepper.
2 oz. salt.
2 qts. water.

Method: Wash, peel and cut the potatoes into small thick lumps. Place half in the bottom of a deep baking tin. Cut the meat the same size, lay it over the potatoes, then the onions minced, and the seasoning. Make the dripping warm in a stew pan and toss the remainder of the potatoes in it; put these on the top of meat, add the water and bake for one and one-half to two hours. Sufficient for fifteen persons.

Hodge Podge.

Ingredients.

1 lb. fresh beef.	1 bay leaf.
1 small carrot.	A little cayenne pepper.
1 small onion.	½ teaspoonful salt.
3 tablespoonfuls cooked green peas.	1 teaspoonful flour.
	1 teaspoonful dripping.
A piece of garlic size of a bean.	½ pint of water.

Method: Cut the meat, carrot and onion into small dice shapes. Brown the onion and meat slightly in the hot fat. Then brown the flour, add the water and stir till smooth. Add the garlic cut finely, the bay leaf and cayenne, and simmer ten minutes, and then strain. Return the gravy to the pan, add the meat, carrot, onions and peas, and simmer for forty minutes before serving.

Beef a la Marine.

Ingredients.

1 lb. salt beef.	¼ teaspoonful pepper.
1 good-sized carrot.	1 teaspoonful vinegar.
1 good-sized turnip.	1 teaspoonful dripping.
1 small onion.	1 teaspoonful flour.
2 cloves.	½ pint water.

Method: Make the dripping hot in the stewpan, and brown the onion and flour in the fat, stir well, and add the water gradually, stirring all the time. Have ready the meat cut into thin fillets, and made fresh by scalding. Add the meat to the gravy, put the carrot and turnip cut into thin strips over the meat, season and simmer one hour.

Peas Pudding.

Ingredients.

1 lb. split peas.	3 leaves of mint.
2 oz. raw salt pork.	¼ teaspoonful pepper.

Method: Tie all the ingredients in a clean cloth, and simmer slowly two hours in plenty of water. Rub through a sieve and brown in oven. Always served with salt pork or boiled bacon.

Plain Suet Pudding.

Ingredients.

6 oz. flour.
6 oz. bread.
3 oz. suet.
½ teaspoonful baking powder.
½ teaspoonful salt.
¼ pint cold water.

Method: Chop the suet finely, removing all skin and fiber. Soak the bread in cold water, then squeeze it well through a clean cloth, and add it to the flour and suet. Mix well together, adding baking powder and salt. Mix all to a smooth dough with water. Put into a well-greased mould and steam two hours.

Molasses Pudding.

Ingredients.

1½ lbs. steeped bread or crew's small biscuits.
1 large tablespoonful molasses.
1 large tablespoonful lime juice.
½ teaspoonful powdered ginger.
1 teaspoonful baking powder
2 tablespoonfuls sugar.
2 oz. suet.

Method: Squeeze the water well out of the bread, put it into a mixing bowl, add molasses, ginger, suet (chopped very fine), sugar, lime or lemon juice, and baking powder. Mix all thoroughly, place in a buttered mould, and steam for two hours. To be served with sweet sauce. The bread is better rubbed through a wire sieve before mixing.

Sea Pie.

(For Ten Men.)

Ingredients.

15 lbs. potatoes.
2 or 3 onions.
1 lb. suet or dripping.
5 lbs. flour.
A little cayenne.
4 lbs. cold salt beef or pork.
2 or 3 carrots or 2 oz. preserved vegetables.
3 quarts water.
1 tablespoonful baking powder.
Salt and pepper.

Method: Peel, and cut up the potatoes, lay in a pan and just cover them with water. Cut up the meat into about half-inch squares, and place it upon the potatoes. Add the chopped onions and sliced vegetables, cayenne, salt and pepper. Set on the fire to boil.

For the Crust: Mix together the flour, salt and baking powder. Add the finely chopped suet, or rub in the dripping if dripping is used. Mix to a stiff paste with cold water; roll it out so as to fit the top of the pan. Lay the crust carefully over the meat and potatoes. Simmer gently two hours.

Plum Pudding.

Ingredients.

1½ lbs. stale bread.
1 oz. candied peel or citron.
6 tablespoonfuls brown sugar.
4 tablespoonfuls finely chopped suet.
Rind and juice of 1 lemon.
6 oz. currants.
6 oz. Valencia raisins.
1 teaspoonful mixed spice.
½ teaspoonful carbonate of soda.

Method: Soak the bread for twenty minutes in cold water. Squeeze it as dry as possible in a clean cloth. Put the bread into a bowl; add the chopped suet, cleaned currants, stoned raisins, and all the other ingredients. Put into a well-greased pudding mould, cover with greased paper and steam for three hours. Serve with sweet sauce flavored with lemon or vanilla.

Yorkshire Pudding.

Ingredients.

1 pint fresh milk.
2 eggs.
¼ lb. flour.
A pinch of salt.

Method: Whip the eggs very lightly, add the milk and salt, pour it gradually onto the flour, and beat it well. Put into a well-greased tin and bake one hour. Pour over it some of the beef dripping, and bake again for ten minutes. Serve it round the beef in slices.

Minced Collops.

2 lbs. lean tender beef.
2 small onions.
½ bunch sweet herbs.
1 large tablespoonful flour.
1 tablespoonful butter.
1 teaspoonful salt.
3 gills of water.
Pepper as required.

Method: Cut the meat and onions finely, sprinkle the herbs over the meat. Fry the onions brown in hot butter, then brown the flour, add the water gradually, and put in the meat and other ingredients. Simmer forty minutes, keeping the pan well covered. Garnish with toasted bread and parsley.

Sausage Rolls.
(Cold Meat Cookery.)

Ingredients.

1 lb. cold meat, fresh, salt or canned.	2 tablespoonfuls soaked bread.
1 ordinary sized onion.	½ teaspoonful pepper.
	Pinch of sweet herbs.

For Pastry.

1½ lbs. flour.	Cold water and salt.
½ lb. dripping or lard.	

Method: Place the flour in the mixing bowl, break the dripping or lard into small lumps and rub them into the flour, add the salt and mix into a dough with cold water. Roll the pastry out twice and leave it to cool. Mince the meat finely, and parboil the onions before mincing them. If salt meat is used, scald it after mincing, add the herbs and seasoning. Mix with the steeped bread well squeezed. Mould into sausages. Lay them on thin sheets of pastry and join the edges by slightly wetting them. Make all the same size and brush over with egg. Bake in a moderate oven one hour.

Beef Brawn.

Ingredients.

4 lbs. shin beef.	½ bunch thyme.
4 bay leaves.	8 pepper corns.
6 cloves.	Salt as required and water.

Method: Cut the meat into one-inch squares, and remove all the fat and gristle. Place it in a stew pan, with enough water to just cover it. Add the herbs, cloves and pepper in a piece of muslin, and simmer slowly for three and one-half hours. Remove the herbs after the first hour. Skim off any fat, taking care not to break the pieces of meat. When tender, add salt, and pour all into a pan or plain mould and leave this to set in a cool place.

Beef Olives.

Ingredients.

2 lbs. rump steak.	1 teaspoonful mixed herbs.
½ lb. bacon.	A little cayenne, also pepper,
2 tablespoonfuls bread crumbs.	and ½ teaspoonful salt.
	1 onion.

Method: Cut the steak into eight thin fillets, as nearly as possible of one size, about two and one-half inches square. Cut the bacon thinly and lay one piece on each fillet. Chop together very finely the trimmings of the meat and the bacon, add the crumbs slightly damped, the herbs, salt, pepper and the finely chopped onion. Put a little of this stuffing on each fillet, and roll them up into sausage shapes. Run two skewers through all to fasten them together, trim the ends and fry them brown in hot fat.

Make one-half pint of brown gravy, nicely seasoned, in a stew pan, lay in the olives, and allow them to simmer slowly for one hour with the pan closely covered. Serve with green olives in the gravy.

Curried Mutton.

Ingredients.

1 lb. mutton.	1 teaspoonful flour.
1 small onion.	1 oz. butter or dripping.
1 large potato or small apple	½ pint water.
1 large tablespoonful curry powder.	Salt as required.

Method: Cut the mutton and potato into pieces the size of a small nut. Make the butter hot in the stewpan and fry the mutton and potato brown. Remove them and leave enough fat in the pan to brown the onion. Add the curry powder and flour, and simmer for one minute, stirring with an iron spoon. Add the water gradually and boil, then add the meat and seasoning, and simmer slowly for forty minutes. One teaspoonful of vinegar and a pinch of sugar improves the flavor.

Scalloped Liver.
(Cold Meat Cookery.)
Ingredients.

1 lb. cold liver.	Spice.
1 small onion.	Salt and pepper.
1 tablespoonful dripping.	¼ pint water.
1 tablespoonful flour.	

Method: Mince the liver and onions small, separately. Make the dripping hot in a stewpan. Brown the onion and flour. Add the water gradually, keeping it well stirred until simmering, then add the liver, herbs, pepper and salt, and simmer slowly for twenty minutes. Serve with sippets of toast.

Rock Cakes.
Ingredients.

1 lb. flour.	1 teaspoonful powdered ginger.
6 oz. lard or good dripping.	
6 oz. sugar.	2 eggs.
4 oz. currants.	1 gill milk or water.
1 large skin of candied peel.	A pinch of salt.
3 teaspoonfuls baking powder.	

Method: Chop one-half of the candied peel, leaving the other for decorating, wash the currants, dry them thoroughly. Mix together all the dry ingredients, make it into a firm dough with the well-beaten eggs and the milk. Drop the mixture on greased pans, in rocky shapes, making about twenty-four cakes. Cut the remaining candied peel into twenty-four thin slices, placing one on each bun, and bake in rather a quick oven for about fifteen minutes.

Soda Scones.
Ingredients.

2 lbs. flour.	powder.
1½ pints fresh milk or water.	½ teaspoonful carbonate of soda.
2 dessertspoonfuls baking	1 teaspoonful salt.

Method: Mix together the flour, salt, baking powder and carbonate of soda. Add the milk or water gradually until sufficient to make a light dough. Handle it as little as possible, and roll out into a large round cake. Mark it deeply into four, brush over with egg, prick with a fork, and place in a hot oven as soon as possible. Time, twenty minutes.

Bubble and Squeak.
(Cold Meat Cookery.)
Ingredients.

2 lbs. cold vegetables (cabbage).
½ lb. bacon.
½ lb. cold beef.
1 small onion.
Pepper, salt.
1 tablespoonful butter.

Method: Chop the vegetables rather finely, slice the onion and brown it in hot butter. Remove the onion, and fry the bacon cut into eight small pieces. Fry the beef lightly in the same way. Lay the slices of beef in the bottom of the dish, place the bacon on the top. Season the vegetables, and fry them in the butter, lay them on the bacon and beef, sprinkle over them the friend onions, and serve very hot.

Vegetarian Department

(Edited by Elizabeth Murray Wardall. All unsigned recipes furnished by the editor.)

Introduction.

Edward Bellamy, giving his picture of the conditions of humanity on earth a hundred years hence, affirms that nothing connected with the customs of the past was so disgusting to the people as the thought that they had ever used flesh as food.

We can quite agree with Bellamy that this will be the case, for even now, when the odors from the slaughter house and the packing plant assail our nostrils, we realize that humanity is only partially civilized, so long as this species of cannibalism continues.

May the time speedily come when we shall know all the lower kingdoms to be prevaded with the same Divine Life that flows through us; when we shall recognize that to the animal we owe a responsibility that is not cancelled by eating his body.

ELIZABETH MURRAY WARDALL.

Hints to Vegetarians.

There is one ingredient that is absolutely necessary to use for those who have banished flesh foods from their cuisine, and that is brain!

If we would secure the nutrition required by the physical body, which has been supplied by animal food, the best of judgment and good common sense must be used, both in the variety and preparation of viands.

I wish to say to housekeepers that if they realized how greatly the work of the kitchen is minimized by non-use of fish, flesh and fowl, to say nothing of the health question, or principle involved, I feel sure they would adopt the vegetarian diet.

All kinds of soups can be prepared much more quickly and with much less work than by using meat stock.

Use those vegetables that blend in flavor, and season to taste with plenty of butter or any of the canned creams.

Nuts are the best and most complete substitute for meat, and walnuts lend themselves to all uses better than others.

Eggs' and cheese are excellent food and can be used in a great variety of dishes.

Macaroni and spaghetti are good foods. Use whole wheat or graham bread.

My experience is that the best oil for pie crust, etc., is a preparation called "Ko-nut," guaranteed free from animal fat. Wesson oil and refined cotton seed oil can also be used.

Both fresh and cooked fruits of all kinds should be used by the vegetarian.

Pickles, neither sour nor sweet, will be craved.

Food For the Sick

(Contributed by R. Mildren Purman, M. D., 305 Globe Building, Seattle, Wash.)

"The measure of a woman is the value she puts on other women."

Especial care should be taken to make the tray which is sent to the sick room attractive, as an invalid's appetite is apt to be small and capricious.

The linen should be fresh and clean, the dishes hot and the portions served should be dainty.

Often it is advisable to give a glass of milk, cup of broth or cocoa, or an eggnog, at 10 a. m. and 3 p. m. in addition to the three small meals given at the usual hours. And a cup of hot milk at bedtime often induces sleep.

No fried foods of any description, hot breads, or veal or pork, with the exception of crisp bacon, should ever be served.

Broths should be allowed to get cold so that all the grease will rise to the top and be removed. If necessary to serve as soon as made, the grease should be entirely removed from the hot broth by soaking it up with unsized brown paper.

Butter and crisp bacon are the only fats allowed. Every particle of fat should be removed from chops and steak before broiling, either in a broiler over coals, or in a pan heated until it smokes, on which the chop is dropped and seared first on one sdie and then the other.

Liquids.

CHICKEN BROTH:

Wash the fowl well. Cut in small pieces. Add one quart of cold water to every pound of meat. Heat slowly to the boiling point and boil gently till the meat is ready to fall from the bones. Strain and skim. If desired, add a tablespoonful of rice and boil for a half hour.

MUTTON BROTH:

One pound neck of mutton washed. One teaspoonful barley, one pint cold water and a little salt. Boil slowly two hours. Strain, cool and skim off the fat.

BEEF TEA:

One pound of round steak cut into dice. Put in covered jar with one pint cold water and a pinch of salt. Soak, stirring occasionally for two hours. Put on the stove in a pan of water and heat gradually, but do not let it reach the boiling point.

OR:

One pound of lean beef cut fine; one pint water and a pinch of salt. Let stand one hour. Put on back of stove and simmer two hours.

BEEF JUICE:

One pound of lean round steak cut into two-inch squares. Sear both sides quickly in a smoking hot, dry pan. Put in beef press or lemon squeezer and press out the juice. Serve cold or barely warm, as heating coagulates the albumen and thus destroys the nutritive quality of the beef.

This is the best way of administering beef: If the patient can be trusted, a tender piece of beef may be seared in the same way after all fat has been removed, and the patient may chew it, swallowing the juice and rejecting the fiber.

BULLION:

Cover one pound of beef cut into small pieces with one pint of cold water and let stand three hours. Put on stove and heat. Strain. Return to kettle and when it boils add the white of one egg beaten with one tablespoonful of cold water and cover quickly. Strain through muslin bag and color with burnt caramel.

FLAXSEED TEA:

One-half cup flaxseed, one quart boiling water. Boil one-half hour and let stand twenty minutes on the back of the range. Strain. If desired, sweeten and add lemon juice.

BARLEY WATER:

Boil two ounces of pearl barley in one and one-half pints water for one-half hour in a covered vessel. Strain. If desired sweeten and add lemon juice.

CORNMEAL GRUEL:

Two tablespoonfuls yellow cornmeal. Add one pint of cold water. Pour off and add one pint of hot milk. Add one-half teaspoonful salt and cook thirty minutes. Serve as it is or with a little sugar and cream.

FLOUR GRUEL:

Heat one pint milk. Moisten two tablespoonfuls flour with a little cold milk and add to the hot milk. Cook twenty minutes. Add a little salt and sugar and nutmeg if desired and serve hot.

ARROWROOT GRUEL:

Heat one pint of milk. Mix one teaspoonful of arrowroot in a little cold milk and add to the hot milk the instant it boils. Add a pinch of salt and cook slowly for ten minutes.

KOUMYSS:

Bring two quarts milk to blood heat. Dissolve one-third cake of compressed yeast in a little lukewarm water. Make a syrup of two tablespoonfuls of sugar and two tablespoonfuls water. Add to milk and stir in yeast.

Put in bottles, not filling them full (or they will burst). Keep in a warm place twelve hours. Lay on the side in a cool place twelve hours (cellar or refrigerator in summer). This will keep twelve hours. Never serve if more than twelve hours old.

ALBUMEN WATER:

Press the white of one egg through a thin clean cloth. Add one-half glass of cold water. If desired, the juice of half a lemon and a teaspoonful of sugar may be added.

EGG AND ORANGE JUICE:

Beat an egg thoroughly with an egg beater. Add finely cracked ice and the juice of two oranges and a teaspoonful of sugar. Mix well and serve.

EGGNOG:

One egg, white and yolk beaten separately; one teaspoonful sugar, one teaspoonful vanilla, one-half glass milk, ice cracked fine. Put the beaten yolk, sugar and four or five small pieces of ice in a glass and beat well. Add a little milk and beat, then add vanilla and the rest of the milk and the beaten white except a little of the white, which should be sweetened and put on top. Brandy should only be used when prescribed by a physician.

COCOA:

One pint of milk simmering in a double boiler, one rounded tablespoonful sugar and two rounded tablespoonfuls cocoa mixed with a little cold milk. Add to the milk and beat well with an egg beater. Take out of double boiler and set on range and boil hard four minutes, stirring constantly. Serve hot.

TEA:

Scald teapot. One teaspoonful of tea to each cup of water. Pour half the quantity of freshly boiled water on the tea and let stand three minutes on the back of stove. Add the rest of the water and serve immediately. Never boil.

COFFEE:

One tablespoonful of coffee to one cup boiling water. Pour the water over the coffee and let stand on back of stove to drip, where it cannot boil, but will keep hot. Pour off and pour over coffee again to drip the second time.

Soup.

CREAM OF POTATO:

Wash and pare a few potatoes. Cover with boiling salted water and cook thirty minutes. Drain and dry on back of stove. Rice them. Melt two tablespoonfuls butter and stir in one tablespoonful flour, add one pint of milk and cook two minutes. Put in double boiler and add one cup of riced potatoes. Cook five minutes, season and serve.

TOMATO BISQUE:

One-half can tomatoes stewed until soft, season and rub through a sieve. Add a saltspoonful of baking soda and when the foaming stops add one tablespoonful of butter. Heat one quart of milk in a double boiler and add a tablespoonful of flour dissolved in a little cold milk, and two tablespoonfuls of butter. Cook ten minutes. Remove from stove and pour into tomatoes. Serve at once.

CREAM OF CELERY:

Cut five heads of celery into inch lengths and cook until tender. Take out and rub through a sieve. Add the celery to one pint of good soup stock and cook slowly one-half hour. Heat one cup of cream and stir into it one tablespoonful of flour rubber into one tablespoonful of butter and cook five minutes. Remove stock and cream from stove and pour together and serve at once.

Eggs.

BOILED FOR TYPHOID PATIENTS:

Warm the egg so the shell will not crack. Put in a pail and pour over it one pint of absolutely boiling water. Cover tightly and statnd on table for five minutes. Open, and egg should be creamy and easy to digest.

SHIRRED EGG:

Break egg into buttered dish and set in hot water and bake two minutes or cook on top of stove till white is jelly like. Season with salt and pepper.

STEAMED EGG:

Drop yolk of egg into a blue cup with a half teaspoonful of butter, a little salt and pepper. Beat the white very stiff, add a very little salt, heap into the cup and cook in boiling water two minutes.

OMELET:

Beat the white of an egg very stiff; add the beaten yolk slowly and a little salt. Put in a hot buttered pan and cook carefully for a minute or two. Fold half over and serve quickly.

BROUILLI:

One-half cup of meat stock heated. Add four unbeaten eggs, four tablespoonfuls cream, salt and pepper. Set the dish in a pan of hot water and cook over a hot fire, stirring constantly, till like a thick jelly. Serve on buttered toast.

Oysters.

PAN ROAST:

Toast a piece of bread, place in the bottom of a baking dish. Cover it with oysters (wiped dry) and season with butter, pepper and salt. Bake until edges of oysters begin to ruffle.

PAN BROIL:

Wipe oysters dry and drop in a hot pan in which a little butter has been melted. Add a little salt and cook till edges of oysters begin to ruffle. Serve immediately. May be served on toast also.

CREAMED OYSTERS:

Wipe twelve large oysters and heat in a pan with a little butter until they ruffle. Have ready a half cup of milk cooked in a double boiler with a rounded teaspoonful of butter and a level teaspoonful of flour until it thickens. Add the oysters as soon as ruffled, season and serve.

BAKED IN SHELLS:

Scrub shells and put in baking pan in hot stove. When the shells open remove the top shell, season with butter, pepper and salt and serve as soon as edges are ruffled.

MACARONI AND OYSTERS:

Break up half a package of macaroni into short lengths and let it boil in salted water until very tender. Drain. Lay the macaroni in a buttered baking dish and sprinkle with salt, pepper and tiny bits of butter. Cover with a layer of oysters and seasoning; then another layer of macaroni and seasoning. Repeat until the dish is full, leaving macaroni on top. Bake in hot oven from four to five minutes.

OYSTERS AND CELERY:

Stew two cups of celery in salted water until transparent and tender. Thicken half a cup of rich milk and pour over the celery. Heat a pint of oysters in their own liquor until the edges curl. Pour into the creamed celery and serve on buttered toast.

OYSTER POULETTE:

Four tablespoonfuls butter, melt and add three tablespoonfuls flour, and one cup oyster juice, and when smooth one cup of cream. eSason with salt, cayenne, and nutmeg. Cool slightly and add the beaten yolks of three eggs and cook slowly till smooth.

Heat one pint of oysters till their edges curl, drop them into the sauce and remove from the fire at once. Serve immediately.

Chicken.

CHICKEN JELLY:

One pound of meat, one pint cold water. Crush bones. Cook slowly until reduced one-half. Season. Strain. Put away in cool place to jelly.

CHICKEN BOUDINS:

One cup chopped cooked chicken, two tablespoonfuls bread crumbs, one-half cup chicken broth, two eggs, salt pepper and a little parsley. Mix all together and beat well. Bake in oven until brown.

CREAMED CHICKEN:

Thicken a cup of rich milk with a tablespoonful of flour and two of butter, season with salt and pepper. Add two cupfuls of cold chicken and cook five minutes. Serve on rounds of buttered toast.

PRESSED CHICKEN:

Boil a chicken until tender; take out all the bones and chop the meat very fine. Season with salt, pepper and plenty of butter. Add to the liquor the chicken was boiled in one cup bread crumbs made soft with hot water, and to this the chopped chicken. When heated take out and press into a mould. Use a weight. Serve cold.

Meat.

RAW BEEF SANDWISH:

Scrape lean round steak with a sharp knife. Spread the scraped meat on thin buttered bread; season with salt and pepper and cover with a piece of thin buttered bread.

SCRAPED BEEF:

Scrape lean round beefsteak, season and make the scraped beef into a little pat and drop on a hot, dry pan. Broil an instant, turn and broil the other side. Serve hot and rare.

STEAK:

Remove all fat and cook over hot coals in a broiler, searing both sides quickly at first and then cooking more slowly afterward, or cook in a hot dry pan. Serve rare.

CHOP:

Remove all fat and trim the bone. Cook in broiler or on a hot dry pan over a good fire four or five minutes.

BIRD:

Singe and draw. Cut down the back and fold legs on breast. Place on a greased broiler. Cook rather slowly with the bone side next to the fire twenty minutes. Just before it is done turn it on the skin side and brown. Season by rubbing with salt and letting it stand one hour before cooking. Serve on toast.

BACON:

Broil in broiler or on a dry pan until very crisp and dry.

Vegetables.

SPINACH:

Wash thoroughly and put on stove in kettle with one or two tablespoonfuls of water. Stir until juices begin to run out. Cook thirty minutes, add salt while cooking. Drain and press through a sieve. Season with salt, pepper and butter.

CREAMED CELERY:

Wash and cut in small pieces; drop in boiling salted water and cook forty minutes. Drain and make a rich thickened milk sauce to pour over it. Season with salt, butter and pepper.

STUFFED POTATO:

Bake a potato. Break open and scrape out the inside. Mash, add salt, pepper and enough cream to make a smooth paste. Beat hard and pack lightly into the potato skins. Return to the oven and brown.

RICE:

Pick over and rub with a cloth one cup of rice. Have ready three quarts of boiling salted water. Sprinkle in rice and cook thirty minutes or until tender without stirring. Drain in a collander and put in open oven about five minutes. Season with salt and butter and serve as a vegetable.

Desserts.

JUNKET:

Heat one pint of milk luke warm. Add two teaspoonfuls sugar and vanilla to flavor. Pour into mould and put where it can stand without being disturbed. Then add two teaspoonfuls Fairchilds' essence of pepsin and stir gently twice. Serve as it is or with cream and sugar.

BLANC MANGE SOUFFLE:

One quart milk, six eggs, six rounded tablespoonfuls sugar, four rounded tablespoonfuls cornstarch. Simmer the milk in a double boiler; add sugar and cornstarch, dissolved in a little cold milk, and cook ten minutes after it thickens. Remove from fire and add the beaten whites, stirring lightly. Flavor with two teaspoonfuls vanilla and put in a wet mould to cool.

SAUCE FOR SOUFFLE:

One and one-half pints milk, four and one-half tablespoonfuls sugar. Heat in double boiler. When it simmers pour over slightly beaten yolks and return to fire and cook till smooth. When cool flavor with vanilla. Serve cold, poured over the souffle.

BAKED CUSTARD (Six Custards):

Melt and brown one-half cup sugar; add two tablespoonfuls hot water. Cover bottom of buttered custard cups.

One pint cold milk, four eggs, two tablespoonfuls sugar. Beat eggs and sugar, add milk, mix well and pour into cups. Stand in hot water and bake twenty to twenty-five minutes in a moderate oven. Turn out at once and serve very cold.

ORANGE CREAM:

½ pint milk.
½ cup sugar.
½ pint whipping cream.
¼ box gelatine (Knox).
3 egg yolks.
Juice of 3 oranges.

Heat milk in double boiler, add gelatine soaked in cold water and stir until dissolved. Beat the sugar and yolks until light, pour the hot milk over them; return to fire and cook two minutes.

Pour into basin, add the juice of three oranges and stand on ice.

When cool, stir in whipped cream; put in wet moulds and put on ice to harden. Serve with cream.

FARINA JELLY:

½ Pint milk. ½ cup suger.
2 level tablespoonfuls farina.

Cook in double boiler fifteen minutes. Pour over one-fourth cup of Knox's gelatine soaked in one-fourth cup of cold water. Add one teaspoonful vanilla, and beat until cool. Add one pint whipped cream, stirring very carefully. Put in wet moulds and serve cold.

TAPIOCA CREAM:

Three tablespoonfuls tapioca covered with water and soaked three hours. Put in double boiler with one quart milk and cook one-half hour.

Beat the yolks of four eggs with one-half cup of sugar and two teaspoonfuls vanilla and stir into tapioca and cook five minutes. Put in buttered baking dish. Beat the whites of the eggs stiff, add four tablespoonfuls pulverized sugar and one teaspoonful of vanilla and drop on tapioca and brown in oven.

SNOW PUDDING:

One-half box Knox's gelatine covered with one-half cup of cold water. Let stand five minutes. Add one pint boiling water and set aside to cool. Add the juice of three lemons and two cups of sugar. When cool beat until white and stiff. Beat the whites of four eggs stiff and add to beaten gelatine and put in moulds to cool. Serve with custard sauce.

CUSTARD SAUCE:

Heat one quart milk in double boiler until it simmers. Pour over the yolks of four eggs beaten with four tablespoonfuls of sugar. Put back in boiler and cook until smooth, stirring constantly to keep from curdling. Flavor with vanilla.

ORANGE PUDDING:

Take five sweet oranges, cut into tiny pieces; lay in pudding dish and cover with one scant cup of sugar.

Boil one pint of milk with a small piece of vanilla bean, a dessert spoonful of sugar and a pinch of salt. Beat the yolks of three eggs with one tablespoonful of cornstarch dissolved in one-half cup of cold milk. Stir into the hot milk and cook until smooth. Let it cool and pour over the oranges.

Beat the whites of the eggs stiff and add one tablespoonful of pulverized sugar, and drop on the pudding and brown delicately in hot oven.

BAKED BANANAS:

Wash bananas and take off a small strip from the side. Loosen the skins, but have them on. Put into a baking pan with a little water. Sprinkle with sugar and baste with orange juice. Bake one-half hour. When done pour over them a little orange juice and set away to cool. Serve cold.

Household Economy and Helpful Hints

"Resolved, That the women of this country ought to be enlightened in regard to the laws under which they live, that they may no longer publish their degradation by declaring themselves satisfied with their present position, nor their ignorance, by asserting that they have all the rights they want."

A Bit of Economy.

In case of any cookies where the sugar has been left out, put the cookies (the baked cookies) through a meat grinder, then add one-half the amount of butter and eggs, a very little flour and enough milk to make the dough roll well.

Dry cake may be utilized in the same way.

MRS. W. L. THOMPSON, Seattle.

Perhaps all housekeepers do not know how good, much better than lard, are beef drippings, that is the fat saved where meat is roasted or stewed. In a large household, if all such fat be saved, the amount spent for lard or cotolene will be greatly lessened.

To Fry Old Fowl That It May Taste Like Spring Chicken.

Dress fowl and cut up in pieces suitable to fry, then season with pepper and salt and roll in flour and drop in pan of boiling lard, turn until nicely browned; pour off most of the lard and put in sufficient water to cover the pieces; set in the oven and bake till the chicken is tender. This can be done with the oldest and toughest fowl and be as nice as spring chicken.

FANNY LEAKE CUMMINGS, M. D.

To Make Two Pounds of Butter Out of One.

This makes real good butter for eating in cool weather when butter is high priced. Take one pound of butter in a vessel and warm until it can be beaten to a cream, then beat into it one pint of tepid sweet milk and the yolk of one egg, adding salt to taste.

If kept in a cool place this is good and goes as far as two pounds of butter. Good for eating only, not cooking.

FANNY LEAKE CUMMINGS, M. D.

To Preserve Breadcrumbs.

Put them in the oven to dry and keep them in a glass jar until needed. The uses of bread crumbs are many; indeed, the breadcrumb jar should hold an important place in the kitchen.

For the breading of cutlets and the making of many kinds of puddings they are indispensible.

MRS. ANDREW OSBERG, LaConner.

Maple Syrup.

Two cups sugar, one teaspoon of mapleine, one cup boiling water. Pour water on the sugar and mapleine and stir until the sugar is all dissolved. Then strain through cheese cloth. Do not cook. This is excellent and will not sugar.

Stale-Bread Hot Cakes.

The most delicious hot cakes that never toughen on cooling. Make batter as for ordinary hot cakes, only thicker and in small amount. Take stale bread and pour boiling water over it and let it stand until the bread is soft; lift out of the water and press out the surplus water; stir gently through the batter and bake as other cakes. These may be tolerated by the most delicate stomach, as they never become tough unless stirred too much in mixing bread into batter.

FANNY LEAKE CUMMINGS, M. D.

Peanut Butter.

Shell a quart of peanuts and remove the skins, pass the peanuts through a meat chopper, grinding them very fine. Add one-fourth pound of good butter and mix with peanut powder, forming a paste, which is ready to spread on thinly sliced bread.

MARIA HAYS McHENRY, Olympia.

To Fry Eggs.

The ordinary fried egg of the restaurant is leathery and indigestible.

Never use lard or butter, but put into your frying pan sufficient bacon or ham fat to cover the bottom a half inch deep. When the fat is hot enough to brown potatoes break the eggs and put in very carefully; with a spoon or pancake turner keep the hot fat running over the tops of the eggs. When done serve immediately on hot plates.

MR. SAVAGE, Seattle.

When frying eggs: Have the butter in the pan melted but not hot; just before placing the pan over the fire add one teaspoon of hot water; cover closely to keep in the steam. The whites of the eggs will be creamy, not hard, when cooked.

In frying meat, if it is inclined to spatter, sprinkle flour over it.

Baked custard will curdle if the oven is too hot. To be sure of a smooth custard set the basin containing it in a pan of hot water.

In boiling dry beans, do not salt them until they are quite soft. Before the beans have softened do not put any cold water into the dish of boiling beans.

If you want a cereal coffee, use barley—the blue barley if it is obtainable—just as you would the real coffee, browning, egging, grinding and boiling. Try it and see how delicious it is.

On taking a pie from the oven, set it on something that will raise it from the table and allow the air to circulate under it, thereby preventing the lower crust from steaming and becoming soggy.

If you are making milk soup or any dish requiring much milk, do not salt it until just as it is served, or the milk will curdle.

By mixing a little milk in the water in which you boil

green corn, you will whiten it and prevent discoloration. Try this and see.

The Holy Stove.

O, the soap-vat is a common thing!
    The pickle tub is low!
The loom and wheel have lost their grace
In falling from their dwelling place
    To mills where all may go!
The bread tray needeth not your love;
    The washtub wide doth roam;
Even the oven free may rove;
But bow ye down to the Holy Stove,
    The Altar of the Home!

Before it bend the worshippers
    And wreaths of parsley twine,
Above it still the incense curls
And a passing train of hired girls
    Do service at the shrine.
We toil to keep the altar crowned
    With dishes new and nice,
And Art and Love and Time and Truth
We offer up, with Health and Youth,
    In daily sacrifice.

Speak not to us of a fairer faith,
    Of a lifetime free from pain—
Our fathers always worshipped here,
Our mothers served this altar drear,
    And still we serve amain.
Our earlier dreams around it cling,
    Birght hopes that childhood sees,
And memory leaves a vista wide
Where mother's doughnuts rank beside
    The thought of Mother's knees.

The woodbox hath no sanctity;
    No glamor gilds the coal;
But the cook stove is a sacred thing
To which a reverent faith we bring
    And serve with heart and soul.
The Home's a temple all divine,

By the Poker and the Hod!
The Holy Stove is the altar fine—
The Holy Stove is the altar fine—
Now, who can be the god?
MRS. CHARLOTE PERKINS GILMAN.

Fireless Cooker.

A very good home-made fireless cooker can be made in the following manner:

Secure a tin box with a telescope cover, large enough to admit a good-sized kettle. This tin box is to be set in a wooden box, sides parallel, and made large enough to allow a space of five inches on all four sides and bottom.

First, fill the wooden box to the depth of five inches with well-packed, finely cut hay, chaff or straw. Set the tin box inside, being sure that the top of the tin box cover comes even with the top of the wooden box. Fill the space around the tin box with the same packing material, and pack it down well.

Fit in boards securely at the top to hold the packing in place. Now make a hollow cover to fit over the top of the wooden box, five inches deep, and fill with the same packing material, allowing for a flange of one inch to slip down over the outside of the wooden box. For convenience put a handle on top of cover and one on each of two opposite sides of the wooden box. Use no hinges. Now the cooker is ready for use.

In preparing a meal, first fill the tin box with boiling water, place a piece of heavy flannel cloth over the top of the cooker and put cover on tightly. Prepare your vegetables and set them to boil on your cook stove in a vessel that will fit the inside of the tin box. As soon as they come to a boil remove the hot water from the cooker and transfer the vessel containing the vegetables into the cooker quickly and cover tightly with the flannel cloth spread over the top of the cooker under the cover.

In five hours the vegetables will be thoroughly cooked, retaining all of their original flavor. It takes two hours longer to cook meats than it does to cook vegetables.

I used a similar cooker one summer while in the mountains, and I assure you it was delightful on returning from a five hours' tramp in the woods to find my dinner nicely cooked, warm and ready to eat.

It saves fuel; keeps the odors of the cooking from circulating through the house; keeps the kitchen many degrees cooler in summer and retains all the original flavor of the vegetables.

EMMA SMITH DeVOE.

We have not deemed it necessary to give receipes for the Fireless Cooker. It is especially adapted for those foods that require long, slow cooking, such as cereals, baked beans, soups, etc.

As one uses it many different dishes will present themselves as best cooked in this manner. As a fuel saver it is an important factor in household economy, and as a means of keeping the house cool during the heated season it is beyond value.

Kitchen Measures.

Ten eggs	One pound
Four kitchen cupfuls	One pound
A pint of liquid	One pound
One cup of butter	One-half pound
One quart of sifted flour	One pound
A teaspoon of liquid	Half ounce
A solid pint of chopped meat	One pound
Three cups of cornmeal	One pound
Two cups of granulated sugar	One pound
A dash of pepper	An eighth of a teaspoonful
Four tablespoons of liquid	One gill or a quarter of cupful

German Cooking

(Contributed by Mrs. Alberta Rouss Janson.)

"The lack of direct political influence constitutes a powerful reason why women's wages have been kept at a minimum."—*Carroll D. Wright, National Commissioner of Labor.*

Sauer Braten.

Take the amount of meat desired for a meal—hare, venison or beef from the rump. Lard the meat by threading a larding needle with fine strips of fat salt pork and drawing through parts of the meat. Into a sufficient quantity of vinegar to cover the meat put a few juniper berries, whole cloves, allspice, bay leaves, dried red peppers, a slice of lemon with rind on, one-half small onion. Place the meat in the pickle and let remain for three or four days, turning each day.

When ready to cook roll the meat in flour, place in pan containing hot fat (lard and butter), brown quickly on all sides. Remove from pan and into the hot fat stir one-half cupful flour and teaspoonful sugar. Strain spices from the vinegar and add it to the gravy. Put meat into gravy and let cook until thoroughly done, adding water as the gravy becomes too thick. Before serving lift out meat and strain gravy into a dish in which has been placed one tablespoonful of sour cream. Serve meat and gravy separately.

Bismarck's Favorite.

Take pieces of tender veal, pork and beef of equal size, cut into dice about half-inch in size. Add one-quarter pound of beef marrow, one onion, one carrot, one turnip cut fine. Place in small, perfectly steam-tight vessel and let simmer until slightly browned, add one-half cupful of water, cover and place on moderately hot fire and let simmer until done, without uncovering. Should cook about an hour.

Wiener Schnitzel (Veal Cutlets).

First dip the cutlet in cold water, salt and pepper, and place on meat board and chop all over with dull, heavy knife, chopping in every direction. Dip in beaten egg and roll in finely chopped bread crumbs. Fry in pan containing sufficient butter and lard in equal proportions to allow for basting. Baste continually while frying.

Kraut Wickel (Cabbage Wrap).

Boil until half done one large cabbage, or remove large leaves and chop small ones. Take one pound each of veal, beef and pork, run through meat cutter and mix some of the finely chopped cabbage, about half as much as meat. Mix and take up a large spoonful of the mixture and place on one of the large cabbage leaves, spreading the meat mixture into a long roll. Roll the leaf into form of a sausage and tie with white thread. Place the rolls in pan with butter and lard. Add a small onion finely chopped. Simmer slowly in covered pan.

Cabbage with Mutton.

Slice a cabbage thin. Put several spoonfuls butter in frying pan. Put in layer of cabbage, layer of mutton, sprinkle over it a few allspice, a little salt and small teaspoonful sugar. Continue the layers alternately, repeating seasoning between each. Use about one teaspoonful allspice to one medium-sized cabbage. A small onion, finely chopped, will also improve the flavor. Add enough water to barely cover bottom of pan. Cover and cook until mutton is thoroughly done.

Blitz Cohn—Lightning Cake.

Six eggs, weigh them and add their weight in sugar, flour equal to weight of four eggs, butter equal to weight of two eggs, grated rind of half lemon.

Beat the yolks and whites of eggs separately until light; add sugar and stir for fifteen minutes. Stir in the sifted flour lightly and stir in partly melted butter and lemon rind. The beating takes the place of baking powder, and if any baking powder is added it should not be more than a teaspoonful.

Butter the pan and sprinkle with toasted, finely rolled

bread crumbs and sliced almonds. Pour in cake batter and sprinkle sliced almonds over top. Bake in moderate oven.

S Cookies.

Three-quarter pound flour, half pound butter, quarter pound sugar. Wash the butter free from salt. Add a pinch of baking powder to flour. One egg, yolks of two more eggs. Put ingredients together in hash bowl and chop lightly until all the flour is taken up by other contents. Take out of bowl onto board. Do not mould or knead with the hands, but press lightly into shape, so it can be rolled. Roll to about one-third inch in thickness and cut in strips about one-half inch wide and three inches long. Bend into shape of an S, lay in pan and bake in moderate oven.

Cookies.

One-half pound flour, one-third pound butter, one-half pound sugar, one whole egg, one yolk, grated rind of one lemon, one tablespoonful sweet cream, small cup finely cut almonds. Chop the ingredients together in chopping bowl, not mixing with the hands. When blended turn out on board and roll about one-quarter inch thick and bake.

Hazelnut Macaroons.

Whites of two large eggs, one-half pound powdered sugar, stirred about fifteen minutes; quarter pound blanched almonds chopped fine; quarter pound hazelnuts chopped fine; pinch of baking powder. Flour the mixing board and roll to about one-half inch thickness.

Prune Pie.

Cut open and remove stones from fresh prunes. Cover pan with dough and arrange the halved prunes, cut side up on dough. Cover with sugar, sprinkle with finely rolled toasted bread crumbs and a light sprinkle of cinnamon, about two tablespoonful melted butter, and bake without a crust.

Zimmersterne (Cinnamon Stars).

Whites of two large eggs, one-half pound powdered sugar, one-half pound unblanched almonds, chopped very fine or ground, one spoonful cinnamon, grated rind of half a lemon. Beat the eggs to a stiff froth. Stir eggs and sugar together for fifteen minutes. Add almonds and small pinch of baking powder. Roll out about one-half inch thick. Cut in stars or small fancy shapes.

Pie Crust.

Take five ounces flour, two ounces butter, one egg, a little milk; mix well together and roll thin.

Lemon Ice.

One quart milk, one pound sugar, grated rind of half a lemon. Let come to a boil in double boiler. Add the juice of six lemons and freeze immediately.

Pudding Sauce.

Four yolks eggs, four tablespoonfuls sugar, one large cup whipped cream. Flavor to taste.

Apple Pie.

Two yolks eggs, three tablespoonfuls sugar, three small potatoes boiled and grated. Stir eggs and sugar light and add potatoes.

Line a pie tin with pie crust or puff paster or a thin layer of shortened raised dough. Spread over the crust a layer of thickly sliced apples. Pour over it the batter and bake.

German Cookies.

One and one-half cup sugar, one cup butter, three eggs, one teaspoonful soda dissolved in hot water, one cup chopped walnuts, one cup chopped seeded raisins, one spoonful cinnamon, flour to make dough stiff enough to roll.

German Pancakes.

Two eggs, one-half pint flour, milk enough to make thin batter a little thicker than cream, one spoonful butter and lard melted, salt. Grease pan and heat well, pour a few spoonfuls of the batter into the hot pan, lift the pan and turn so that batter spreads over entire bottom, then pour off all except thin layer that adheres to bottom of pan. Return pan to fire and let cake brown on both sides. Put on heated plate, cover with jelly or syrup and roll. To be eaten immediately.

Miscellaneous

Chestnut Cream Soup.

One quart of milk, three tablespoonfuls flour, three tablespoonfuls butter, one pound chestnuts blanched, boiled and mashed. Flavor with a little onion juice and salt and nutmeg if desired. A spoonful of whipped cream added just before serving improves the taste and appearance.

Puree of Sweet Potatoes.

Six medium-sized sweet potatoes, boiled and pressed through a vegetable press or mashed. One quart of milk, one pint of chicken stock. Salt and butter to taste, and if liked a little mace. A cup of whipped cream added just before serving will greatly improve the flavor.

Spiced Beef Appetizer.

Prepare a spiced vinegar as for fruit pickles, only less highly seasoned. Cut very, very thin slices of dried beef in ornamental shapes—narrow strips, diamonds, etc., are easily cut with scissors. Steam the beef in the vinegar for one hour. Serve hot with toasted wafers.—A. S., in Good Housekeeper.

(A trial proves this recipe so very good that a special indorsement is added, lest it be rejected because so unusual. —The Editors Good Housekeeper.)

Tomatoes Stuffed with Succotash.

Wash, wipe and remove a thin slice from the stem end of six uniform-sized tomatoes, scoop out the inside, sprinkle with salt, invert, let stand one-half hour. Mix the pulp with one cup of succotash; stuff tomatoes and arrange them in a granite dripping pan, well buttered. Sprinkle the top of each with buttered cracker crumbs. Bake in a hot oven twenty minutes or until tender. Baste with melted butter.

Mayonnaise Dressing.

1 teaspoonful mustard.
1 teaspoonful powdered sugar.
½ teaspoonful salt.
¼ salt spoonful cayenne.

Yolks of two raw eggs.
1 pint olive oil.
2 tablespoonful vinegar.
2 tablespoonful lemon juice.

Mix the first four ingredients in a bowl, add the eggs, stir well with a spoon. Stir a little of the oil and if it thickens then add a little lemon juice. Then a little oil and then a little vinegar. By this time it will be thick and you can add much oil and the vinegar in limited amounts. We stir ours up with a dover egg. Later, not necessary to add the material drop at time provided the first thickens. We usually do not put in the full amount of sugar or of mustard. We never put in the full amount of sugar when the dressing is to be used for a meat salad.

For our family we often halve the recipe, but in winter it keeps so well that we sometimes make all. The oil does not want to be too cold in winter and the ingredients and dishes must all be cold in summer. I always put the egg, lemon and dishes on the ice in summer. If it does not thicken, take a new yolk, beat a little and add the mixture.

HARRIETT TAYLOR UPTON.

Mrs. Thompson's Johnny Cake.

Cream together butter size of a walnut, pinch of salt and two tablespoons sugar. Add one egg and beat all together. One and one-quarter teaspoonsful baking powder, three-quarters cup of yellow meal and one and one-quarter cups white flour. Milk to make thin batter.

Brown Bread.

One cup molasses, one teaspoonful salt, one heaping spoon soda, two cups sweet milk and one of sour milk, three cups cornmeal and one of flour. Mix in order named. Steam three hours.

Mrs. Kendall's Johnny Cake.

One egg, one teaspoon salt, two tablespoon sugar, one cup of milk, one cup of cornmeal and one cup of flour, sifted together. Blueberries added if obtainable.

Rolled Oats Rolls.

Two cups rolled oats. Put to soak over night in one and one-half cups sour milk. In the morning add one beaten egg, one tablespoon sugar, one teaspoon soda, salt and three-quarters cup flour.

MRS. PURINGTON.

Billie's Brown Bread.

Three cups graham flour, coarse; two cups sour milk, one cup molasses, two level teaspoons soda in a little hot water, pinch of salt, one-half cup seeded raisins. Steam three hours.

MISS CONLON.

Mayonnaise Dressing.

One cupful of olive oil, yolks of five eggs, whites of three eggs (yolks and whites beaten separately), one level teaspoonful of powdered sugar, pinch of cayenne or paprica, one teaspoonful salt.

Boil in double cooker, stirring constantly until a thick custard.

Let cool. Place in pan of cold water to hasten cooling. When cold add one cupful of olive oil, a little at a time, beating it all the time with a Dover egg beater.

EMMA B. SMITH.

Cheese Fondue.

Soak one cup of bread crumbs in two cups milk. Three eggs, beaten lightly, half tablespoonful melted butter, pepper and salt to taste. Add last two cups grated cheese. Mix altogether and bake until brown.

Or one cup bread crumbs soaked in two cups milk. One cup grated cheese, salt and pepper. Mix altogether and bake until brown on top. Serve immediately.

EMMA B. SMITH.

Fruit and Vegetables.

Two medium-sized apples, four good-sized stalks of celery, one carrot, small head of lettuce, one orange, one tablespoonful of sugar. Chop fruit and vegetables and serve on lettuce leaf with mayonnaise dressing.

Fruit and Nuts.

One good-sized stalk of celery, two-thirds cup of walnuts, one apple, one carrot. Chop rather fine and serve with mayonnaise on lettuce leaf.

MRS. J. G. MARX.

Fruit and Nuts.

One-half banana, sliced lengthwise; one-quarter orange, one-quarter apple and one tablespoonful English walnuts chopped rather fine. Serve on lettuce leaf with whipped cream. Enough for one person.

Spanish or Mexican Beans.

Two pounds of Bayo beans, one pound salt pork or ham bone, one onion, one heaping tablespoonful of Eagle Chili powder. Soak beans over night, drain, mix all together, cover well with water and cook slowly for four hours. Salt and pepper to taste.

Baked Potatoes.

Select potatoes of a uniform and medium size. Wash them well and drop them in boiling water, into which has been added a pinch of soda. Boil four or or five minutes according to the size. Take out and put in hot oven and bake until brown.

MRS. CLARA RIPLEY SMITH.

Potato Peanuts.

Soften two tablespoons of peanut butter with a little boiling water and add it to one cup of hot, mashed potatoes, seasoning liberally and beating until light. Shape into four flat cakes. Flour lightly and brown in a little hot fat. Just before serving, pour over them a hot tomato sauce made by sifting and slightly thickening a cup of canned tomatoes, well seasoned. Or they may be served without sauce, garnished with parsley.

Pepper Cups.

Slice off the tips from as many small, ripe peppers as you have guests, remove the seeds and boil twenty minutes in salted water containing a dash of vinegar. Drain, stand them upright and fill with minced chicken or veal, prepared with seasoned stock as for jellied chicken. Set on ice to harden, placing a spray of curled parsley in the top of each for a garnish, or the caps may be boiled separately and replaced if preferred.

Olive oil used as a substitute for butter in seasoning string beans, summer squash, macaroni and many other dishes gives a bland rich flavor much appreciated.

Sandwich Fillings.

Equal parts of boned and skinned sardines and cream cheese mashed to a pulp together produce a combination which tastes almost exactly like goose liver pate and is much cheaper and not as indigestible. Chipped beef, chopped very fine and mixed with mayonnaise, is a simple, inexpensive and delicious sandwish filling. No one would ever be able to identify the chipped beef. It tastes much like chopped ham. —M. C. D., in Good Housekeeping.

Salmon Loaf with Rice.

One can salmon flaked or equal quantity fresh salmon boiled in salt water, two cups hot boiled rice (one cup raw rice makes the right quantity), two eggs beaten, two tablespoonfuls melted butter, juice of half small lemon, salt and pepper to taste. Add liquor from salmon can. Mix lightly with fork. Bake in covered pan set in water one and one-half hours in moderate oven. Serve with drawn butter sauce, made from half cup butter, two tablespoonfuls flour, one pint of water. Melt butter, stir in flour, pour in one pint boiling water and boil till clear. Turn loaf out on platter and pour sauce over it.

MRS. EMMA B. SMITH.

Salmon Loaf Steamed.

One can salmon or equal quantity fresh salmon boiled in salt water, two eggs, half cup milk, four tablespoonfuls melted butter, salt and pepper to taste, two cups bread crumbs. Steam in covered buttered dish one hour.

Dressing—One cup milk, one tablespoonful cornstarch, two tablespoonfuls melted butter, one egg. Scald the milk, add cornstarch, butter and eggs. Cook one minute. Add liquor from can. Turn salmon loaf on platter and pour the dressing over it.

MRS. EMMA B. SMITH.

Hungarian Stew for Five Persons.

Cut two pounds of good lean roundsteak, porterhouse or sirloin without bones into one one-half inch squares. Chop a big onion into small pieces and brown these in two big tablespoonfuls of fine lard in a deep vessel. Then add salt, a small tablespoonful of paprica and the meat. Cover the pot and let it cook until the meat is half done, always adding enough water to keep it from burning.

Peel and cut meanwhile eight to ten moderately sized potatoes into squares and add them to the meat when half done. Cover the whole with about three inches of water and cook till the potatoes are soft. By that time the meat must be done and the gravy ought to have the consistency of good cream. Serve immediately.

Pressed Meat.

Take three pounds beef neck, boil until very tender in plenty of water; take out of liquor and set away to cool.

Into the liquor put one cup of rolled oats or a little less quantity of cream of wheat, boiled into a jelly.

Chop meat with onion and parsley, according to taste, then mix chopped meat and the jelly together, season with salt and pepper to taste. Press in bread tins and set in oven five or ten minutes to brown. Set away for cold sliced meat.

MISS EMMA S. WOOD.

Summer Mince Meat.

1 peck green tomatoes.	2 tablespoonsful cinnamon.
2 lbs. raisins.	2 tablespoonsful allspice.
4 lbs. brown sugar.	Juice 4 lemons.
2 cups suet.	Chopped rind 2 lemons.
1 tablespoonful salt.	

Chop tomatoes and let them drain. Put them in kettle with cold water enough to cover. Let come to a boil. Drain again. Then add suet and raisins. Cook thoroughly. Add one-half cup vinegar and the spices. Cook a little. Can while hot. Makes six quarts.

MRS. EMMA B. SMITH.

To Crack Pecans.

Pour boiling water over the pecans and let them cool in the water. Strike the small ends in cracking and salt as you would almonds.

Pineapples, How to Cut.

The toughness of pineapples is almost entirely eliminated by slicing the fruit up and down from stem to blossom ends instead of through the core. Thrust the fork into the blossom end to hold the pineapple steady, and slice until you come to the hard, pithy core, which can then be discarded.—Old Pineapple Grower.

Chestnut Cakes.

Beat the yolks of eight eggs until very light and add to them the finely chopped meats from one-half pound of mixed nuts. Beat the whites of the eggs, and when stiff fold in lightly the puree from a pound of chestnuts. Cut and fold the yolks into the whites, add one-half teaspoon of vanilla. Bake in small pans in a slow oven for forty minutes.

Chestnut Glace.

Two cups of sugar, one cup of water and a pinch of cream of tartar boiled until it takes on a slight amber tinge. Have the chestnuts shelled and blanched and dip them into the hot syrup, using a hat pin or sharp wooden skewer to lift them.

How to Carve

The first essential in carving, indeed the very foundation of all good work in this respect, is knowledge of the relative position of bones, joints, fat and muscles. It is an easy matter to cut straight and neatly a solid mass of meat, but it is quite another thing to carve scientifically a roast fowl or game with the bones still in place. So the first thing to be mastered is the anatomy of the joint or bird, and to thoroughly understand the direction in which the muscular fibers run. When this is accomplished more than half the work of carving is done.

A cool head, control of one's temper, a sharp knife, a seat of the right height, plenty of room, and a dish of sufficient size are of secondary importance, but all very necessary to rapid and graceful carving.

The knife, a most important element in good carving, should always be well sharpened on a steel before being brought to table—and it is good economy to have special knives for different meats. Use a long, broad-bladed knife for roast beef and all large joints. For poultry and small joints a smaller narrow-bladed knife should be used.

To Carve Roast Turkey.

Place the fork in the breast of the turkey, one prong being on each side of the bone. Grasp the handle of the fork with the left hand, and laying the flat of the knife (held in the right hand) parallel with, and close to, the neck, just above where the left wing joins the body; cut downward, reaching the joint. A slight pressure severs the cartilage, and a single sweep of the knife removes the wing.

To remove the left leg and second joint, put the knife into the flesh which holds the second joint, cut downward to the point where the second joint joins the carcass. Place the knife between the leg and the carcass, and make a downward sweep. A gentle pressure with the point of the knife will cause the leg and second joint to drop off. The breast should then be sliced, the slices running parallel with the breast-bone, and being cut wide and long and not too thin.

Next cut out the oyster bone by placing the flat of the knife against the vertebrae connecting the "Pope's nose" with the carcass, and press the edge of the knife in the direction of the bird's neck, then turn the blade, and the leverage causes the oyster bone to fall into the dish. After removing the oyster bone, turn the dish and take off the right wing, leg, breast and oyster bone in the same way as on the left.

To remove the wish bone place the flat of the knife against the breast bone, and, keeping it pressed against the carcass, sweep it toward the neck. The breast bone must be moved last of all, as the fork is never taken out of it until that bone comes to be separated from the carcass.

Roast Chicken.

The directions given for carving roast turkey will also answer generally for roast chicken, except that the legs, being smaller, are not divided into so many parts.

Roast Duck.

Place the duck on the dish with the head at the left; insert the fork firmly across the ridge of the breast bone, and, beginning at the wing, cut the meat in long thin fillets parallel with the breast bone. The rest of the bird may be cut up in the same way as roast chicken.

Roast Goose.

Place the goose in the same position as the duck and carve in the same way. Never attempt to carve a goose as you would a turkey, as this always proves disastrous. Begin at the wing and cut down through the meat to the bone the entire length of the breast. Cut this until the ridge of the breast bone is reached, then remove the slices from the bone and cut the other side of the breast in the same way. Cut off the wing at the joint, tip the body over slightly, and cut off the leg. The wish bone, shoulder blade and collar bone may then be treated in the same way as in a turkey.

Shoulder of Mutton.

Place the shoulder on edge and cut slices from the top edge. These at first are mostly fat, and some of them should be served with lean cuts. Cut thin slices from the part above the knuckle and down to it. Then place the joint flat on the platter and slice from both sides of the blade bone. After removing this bone cut up the remainder, being careful to cut across the grain. One of the important points in carving mutton is to carve rapidly so that it may be served hot.

Sirloin of Beef.

In carving sirloin of beef first cut close to the back bone, straight down to the spine, slip the knife between the spine and the meat, and then cut into thin slices, serving a small piece of crisp fat with each helping.

Leg of Veal.

The hip bone should be removed before the leg is cooked. Place the joint on a dish with the thicker end to the right; carve slices from the thickest side of the leg bone first, and then from the other side. This will keep the face of the joint almost even.

Tongue.

The tip of the tongue being not so juicy as the thicker part should be carved first, as if left a day or so becomes dry and indigestible. Trim off the ragged thick end and remove the little bones, then slice as thin as possible, serving a slice of the thick part and a slice of the tip together.

Tables

Proportions.

5 to 8 eggs to 1 quart of milk for custards.
3 to 4 eggs to 1 pint of milk for custards.
1 saltspoonful of salt to 1 quart of milk for custards.
1 teaspoonful of vanila to 1 quart of milk for custards.
2 ounces of gelatine to 1¾ quarts of liquid.
4 heaping teaspoonfuls cornstarch to 1 quart of milk.
3 heaping teaspoonfuls of baking powder to 1 quart of flour.
1 teaspoonful of soda to 1 pint of sour milk.
1 teaspoonful of soda to 1 pint of molasses.
1 even teaspoonful of baking powder to 1 cup of flour.
1 teaspoonful of baking powder is the equivalent of ½ teaspoonful of soda and 1 teaspoonful of cream of tartar.

Tables of Weights and Measures.

4 gills=1 pint.
2 pints=1 quart.
4 quarts=1 gallon.
16 ounces=1 pound.

½ kitchen cupful=1 gill.
1 kitchen cupful=½ pint, or 2 gills.
4 kitchen cupfuls=1 quart.

2 cupfuls of granulated sugar or 2½ cupfuls of powdered sugar = 1 pound.
1 heaping teaspoonful of sugar = 1 ounce.
1 cupful of butter = ½ pound.
4 cupfuls of flour or 1 heaping quart = 1 pound.
1 heaping teaspoonful of butter, or butter the size of an egg = 2 ounces, or ¼ cup.
8 round teaspoonfuls of dry material or 16 teaspoonfuls of liquid = 1 cupful.

Time Table for Boiling Meats and Fish.

MEATS—		Time.
Mutton	Per lb.	15 min.
Potted Beef	"	30 to 35 min.
Corned Beef	"	30 min.
Ham	"	18 to 20 min.
Turkey	"	15 min.

Chicken	"	15 min.
Fowl	"	20 to 30 min.
Tripe	"	3 to 5 hours.
FISH—		Time.
Codfish	Per lb.	6 min.
Haddock	"	6 min.
Halibut	"	15 min.
Blue	"	10 min.
Bass	"	10 min.
Salmon	"	10 to 15 min.
Small Fish	"	6 min.
Lobster	"	30 to 40 min.

Household Department

To prevent eyeglasses from steaming in cold weather, rub the glasses thoroughly on both sides with a little vaseline or cold cream, then rub with tissue paper or cloth to clear the glasses. Glasses treated this way will not cloud or steam in the coldest weather for twenty-four hours. This treatment of the glasses should be made once a day for outdoor use.

To Boil Water Without Burning.

To boil water without burning is a clever thing to do. Water to be palatable and healthy should only just come to a boil; that is, to the boiling point, then set aside, where it can be kept at this point until wanted for use.

Water that is kept boiling soon losses its best flavor in the evaporation, and this leaves the old burnt material in the teakettle, and such water is not fit to drink.

MRS. JENNIE JEWETT, White Salmon.

Hard Soap for Laundry and Kitchen.

Dissolve one can Babbit's lye or potash and one-half cup of borax in three and one-half pints of cold water at night, in a granite ware or iron kettle. Dissolve borax in the water before adding the lye. The next morning put five pounds of grease saved from cooking bacon, etc., in a kettle and bring it to a blood heat; put in one-half cup of ammonia, then add grease to the lye (not the lye into the grease) slowly, stirring until it thickens to the consistency of honey. Just as it begins to thicken add 10 cents' worth oil of sassafrass. Pour into a mould and let stand twenty-four hours in a cool place to harden. Cut in any size bars you wish. It improves with age. A convenient mould is found in paper cracker boxes, lining them with the oiled paper greased.

MRS. EMMA B. SMITH.

Cleaning and Laundry.

If spots on goods are obstinate in refusing to yield to usual methods, try them with a mixture of ammonia and gasoline.

Sweeping—Wet newspapers, squeeze out all water possible, tear into small pieces and scatter over the carpets before sweeping them. You will be surprised to see how nicely the papers clean them.

Wash the table silver in hot, clean soap suds, wiping directly from the suds without draining, and they will rarely need polishing.

When handkerchiefs get dingy, as they are apt to, boil them in blue water, and you will be surprised to see how it will whiten them.

Never set a nickle-plated article directly over the flame of a gas stove. Place a protecting plate between.

Copper and brass may be quickly cleaned by dipping half a lemon in fine salt, and then rubbing over the stained objects, afterwards washing in warm water.

Stains caused by sewing machine oil can be removed by dampening with liquid ammonia before washing.

Equal parts of olive oil and vinegar makes a good furniture polish and will remove white stains caused by heat and hide scratches.

Cover a grease spot on matting with French chalk and sprinkle with benzine. Allow the benzine to evaporate and brush off the chalk and the grease spot will have disappeared.

Renovating Fluid.—One gallon deodorized gasoline, two ounces alcohol, four ounces sulphuric ether, one-half ounce oil of wintergreen, one-fourth ounce lavender oil, pulverized borax one dram. Keep corked tight to prevent evaporation.

MRS. C. E. FERGUSON, Columbia City.

Making and Applying Wood Stains.

With the spirit of home-decoration that in these days is so general, much is missed by lack of knowledge in regard to wood stains and their preparation. This ignorance is not confined entirely to housekeepers, but prevails with many so-called professional painters. Many articles of furniture, as well as floors, can be much improved in appearance by the use of stains.

A beautiful stain when properly prepared can be made from any of the following pigments, viz: Raw and burnt sienna, raw and burnt umber and Vandyke brown. Besides the foregoing, carmine, crimson lake and American vermillion can be used to an advantage when prepared as directed below.

To make a stain from any of the materials named above it is best to buy it "ground in oil," for the reason that when mixed in the dry state it is liable to be grittey and does not produce as good an effect.

The writer's experience in making stains of any shade is that if the material is first mixed with a sufficient quantity of raw linseed oil to make it the consistency of thick cream, and then slowly brought to a boil over a moderate fire, and while boiling add a piece of yellow beeswax (in the proportion of a piece about the size of half a nutmeg to a pint) and allow to boil until the wax is melted and thoroughly mixed with the material, the stain has a better effect and lasts longer. After removing from the fire allow the mixture to stand a few minutes, and then thin with turpentine to whatever consistency you desire. Under no circumstances, however, should the turpentine be put in until after the boiling, as the presence of the latter would make the mixture very liable to take fire and probably endanger the maker's safety.

Raw sienna as a stain produces a beautiful shade of yellow. Burnt sienna, when properly thinned, produces a very nice mahogany shade, and in combination with red oxide of lead does very well for a cherry stain. Either burnt umber or Vandyke brown will make an excellent black walnut stain. Raw umber makes a stain that some persons prefer to all others for floors. Carmine, when combined with burnt sienna, produces a beautifully brilliant stain, between a mahogany and a cherry. Crimson lake produces a beautiful rose color when properly diluted, and has an admirable effect when applied to the floor extending out from the washboards about eight inches around a room, having all the balance of the floor inside this border stained with raw sienna. It makes everything look cool and refreshing even on a sultry day. American vermillion when used as a stain should be very thin, and produces on a new, even surface a lovely deep pink.

To obtain the best results from any stain, it should be varnished, but never until it is thoroughly dry. To apply any of the cheap, ordinary varnishes, which are made from rosin and other inferior materials, is a waste of money as well as time and labor.

A No. 1 hard oil finish is the proper varnish to apply.

If you desire a very brilliant gloss, thin the finish with about a gill of raw linseed oil to a quart of the varnish. It is a quick dryer and in twelve hours, in warm weather, it will be dry. Never apply the finish just as you buy it, as generally it is too heavy (thick) to spread evenly. Floors that have been stained and varnished with hard oil finish can from time to time be freshened up, when the gloss begins to die away, by going over the floor with some raw linseed oil, in which has been melted, by boiling, some yellow beeswax, in the proportion of half an ounce of wax to three pints of oil.—Selected.

To obviate the trouble which often arises from trying to use dishes on the gas range too small to fit the racks, cut squares from wire window screening to fit over the space and set the dishes upon it.

Any housekeeper, especially one who entertains a great deal, will find a serving wagon of great assistance. This can easily be made at home by putting casters on a sewing table and fastening strips of molding around the edge to prevent dishes falling off. A great many more soiled dishes can be piled upon it than can be carried out with the hands, and if a large enough table is selected an entire course can be brought in at one trip.

In addition to this, a little serving table placed within convenient reach of the hostess may be utilized to advantage. From it may be served the salad course, with its accompaniment of cheese and crackers, such relishes as celery, olives and the like, fruit, nuts and raisins. Bonbons and various candies would also find their place here, in addition to a coffee percolator with its following of cream pitcher, sugar bowl and cups and saucers. In this way the coffee could be made right at the table, kept warm until wanted, and served without the hostess being obliged to so much as rise from her seat.

Any table large enough will do for this purpose. If you have no serving table proper, and concealed under a pretty luncheon cloth will look every bit as well as the most handsome bit of furniture that the shops have to offer.

Hints For Beauty and Hygiene

Cucumber Cream.

Two ounces cucumber juice, one ounce white wax, one ounce spermactei, four ounces almond oil, one ounce orange flower water.

Put the oil in a double boiler and when warm add cucumber after washing and chopping fine. Take large ripe ones and do not peel them. Let oil and cucumbers simmer for two hours. Add the wax, spermacetti and the orange flower water until it is creamy. Keep in a tight box.

For Rough and Cracked Skin.

Equal parts of glycerine and egg albumin. Perfume this cream as you wish—a few drops of perfume.

To Whiten Complexion.

Mix a handful of well-sifted wheat bran with a pint of white vinegar. Let stand for four hours. Add the yolks of five eggs. Put into a bottle and keep corked fifteen days. This lotion may be applied to the face at night.

Nail Paste.

One drachm powdered carmine (fine), two ounces fresh lard, twenty-four drops oil of Bergamot, twelve drops essence of cypress.

Beat well together and heat in a double boiler, stir them to a smooth paste. To avoid staining the fingers apply the paste with a bit of old linen. Let remain a few minutes, then wipe off.

Hand Lotion.

One hundred and two ounces quince seed, half pint bay rum, four ounces rose water, one hundred and two pints distilled or soft water, two ounces glycerine, juice of two lemons.

Pour water over quince seeds and let them stand over night, then strain and add other ingredients.

MARTHA G. RIPLEY, M. D.

To Keep Hands Free from Stain.

Keep a bottle of peroxide of hydrogen and ammonia in the kitchen during the summer months. This will clean the hands and nails from unsightly fruit stains, especially berry stains. Raw tomatoes are good for the purpose, but the recipe is the better.

MRS. CLARA RIPLEY SMITH.

Hair Remover.

Sulphide of barium, 31 SS.; oxide of zinc, 3 VI.; carmine, Gr. 1.

Some of this powder is to be mixed with enough water to make a paste. Apply to the parts and wash off in three minutes.

MRS. ABIGAIL RIPLEY SMITH.

Cold Cream.

Two ounces almond oil, one ounce cocoa butter, one ounce spermacetti or white wax, two ounces rose water.

Pour the oil into a bowl and cut the butter and wax into it. Place the bowl in a dish of hot water and set on stove until the ingredients are entirely melted. Remove and let slightly cool, but not harden. Have the rose water cold and beat the oil with an egg beater or silver fork, adding the rose water a spoonful at a time until all is added. The mixture should be creamy and very soft and refreshing to the face. A good skin food.

MAY GRINNELL.

Nail Powder.

Violet talcum powder, one-half ounce; boric acid (pulverized), one-half ounce; powdered starch, one-half ounce; tincture of carmine, fifteen drops.

For Red Hands.

Honey, one ounce; almond oil, one ounce; juice of one lemon, yolk of one egg. Mix well.

Tooth Wash.

Liquid.—Peppermint, 15 drops; alcohol, one-half ounce; rose water, one ounce; tincture of orris, one-half ounce.

Toilet Water.

Alcohol, one pint; orange flower water, one ounce; essence of bergamot, two drachms; essense of lemon, one drachm; oil of neroli, twenty drops; oil of rosemary, six drops.

These ingredients, after being thoroughly mixed, are put into a bottle and tightly corked.

Carnation Toilet Water.

Oil of pink, one ounce; rectified spirits, one pint.

Menthol Vinegar Makes a Good Headache Cologne.

Three parts menthol, ninety-seven parts of white vinegar.

Lotion for Bunions.

Glycerine, two drachms; carbolic acid, two drachms; tincture of iodine, two drachms.

This is to be applied every day with a camel's-hair brush pencil.

Powder for the Feet.

Tannin, thirty drachms; lycopodium, three drachms; alum, one drachm.

Good Shampoo.

Dry Shampoo.—Take the finest ground white cornmeal, add a little powdered orris root and sprinkle the powder through the hair. Massage the scalp and rub the powder over it. Shake the powder through the long hair, letting it stand for half an hour. Remove the meal from the hair with a long fibred brush.

Cold Cream.

Melt together until soft: White wax, one ounce; sweet almond oil, two ounces; cocoanut oil, one ounce; benzoin, one-half ounce.

When the ingredients will amalgamate well, whip them with a fork until cold and of a cream-like consistency. Before whipping add a few drops of bergamot or rose water.

Hints on Breathing.

The majority of people are too lazy to breathe; that is, to breathe properly and sufficiently. They get along with just as little air as possible, go blocks out of their way to avoid climbing a hill, and by so doing they never experience the exhilarating influence of deep, diaphragmatic breathing. If they run for a street car they blow and wheeze like a wind-broken horse. It is strange how one will economize on air, the cheapest thing in the world.

Don't be afraid to breathe the night air. It is the only air you can get at night except the vitiated air of a close room.

Hints on Bathing.

The drinking of an abundance of water, and the daily bath are actually essential to thorough cleanliness and health.

A daily before breakfast cold-water bath (tub, hand or shower) should be taken by everyone having sufficient vitality for re-action; if not, then tepid or warm water bath (not hot).

Hot-water tub baths should be avoided by the thin-blooded, neuralgic and very nervous person. If such a bath is taken it should be just before retiring. End a hot-water bath with a cold plunge or splash.

Never taken cold-water bath when fatigued, but a warm-water bath is restful.

Do not take any kind of bath directly after a hearty meal.

Do not take a warm or hot-water bath in a cold room. It will invariably be followed by a chilling sensation.

Do not exercise after, but before, bathing. If you have to exercise to get warm after a cold-water bath, it is a sure indication that your vitality is too low for such a bath.

A cold-water bath in a cold room (for one with sufficient vitality) is a positive luxury.

Children, especially, should have daily baths and frequent changes of underclothing.

Health Exercise.

It should be borne in mind that physical exercises of some kind should be taken daily by everyone. The end or aim of all exercises should be, primarily, health. The fewer exercises the better, and then have them for a specified object. All exercises should be taken regularly daily; not as an irksome duty, but with the thought of health and strength. In the various employments of both men and women, the arms and legs receive more exercise than the trunk of the body. The trunk of the body contains the vital organs. It is to the strengthening of these that we must look for the freedom from disease.

What to Do on Arising.

First—Get all the pure air you can.

Second—Cleanse the teeth, rinse the mouth and gargle.

Third—Drink one or more glasses of cold water (not ice water; no, not hot water—too relaxing and no tonic effect). If constipated, put a teaspoonful of salt in the first glass of water. Omit the salt when no longer needed.

Exercise No. 1—Bend as far forward as possible without bending the knees. Keep the head up, and thus prevent dizziness.

Bend as far backward as you can without undue strain or losing your balance.

Be sure to bend the knees when going backward. Begin with the hands at the waist, but as soon "as you get the hang o' the thing," raise your hands high and swing your arms back over the head as you bend backward, then swing forward with all the stretch (upward and forward) that you can put into the movement.

Inhale as you swing the arms up and back, exhale as you swing them forward. Try to touch the tips of the fingers to the floor (without bending the knees).

Begin with five times (forward and back, counting one), continue gradually until you reach fifty.

Exercise No. 2—Stand erectly and firmly on both feet. Grasp an imaginary dumb-bell in each hand. Swing the right arm out to the side and high up over the head. Stretch the side muscles to the utmost as you swing the arm upward. As the right arm descends to the lowest possible point (without yielding anywhere but the waist) the left arm should swing out and up to the highest stretching point. Do not turn nor twist the body nor lean forward. Do not hold the breath, but inhale and exhale naturally. Begin with five times (both sides counting one). Continue gradually until you reach twenty-five.

Exercise No. 3—The "liver squeezer" consists of turning or twisting the body right and left, while otherwise retaining the body in an erect position. Do not allow the feet to move, nor the body to bend either forward or backward. Avoid jerking, but when going as far each way as possible, without straining, give just a little extra, steady pull as if to go "just a little farther." Begin with five (counting both ways one) and continue gradually until you reach fifteen.

Be as regular in these exercises as you are in your devotions; no, no, that will not do. Be as regular as you should be in your devotions.

Think of the benefit, the cleansing, the toning up that your stomach is getting by its internal bath during your exercises. I am sure if it could speak to you it would say: "I am so grateful."

Following these three exercises with a bath, either a tub or shower or hand (cold, cool, tepid or warm, preferably cold, or warm followed with cold). Follow the water bath with an air or sun and air bath.

Takes too much time? Only about twenty minutes when you get accustomed to it. Cut your morning nap a little short. It will pay you an excellent dividend for the time invested.

Is that all the exercise needed? That's all, and that's enough for the average person, if faithfully followed.

Science in the Kitchen.

The kitchen is the laboratory in which is compounded the life-sustaining elements by which the members of the family are nourished and equipped for the duties of life. It is the most important department of the home, and the home is the most important factor in the nation. The progress of civilization is traced by the advance of industrialism; and the first object of industrialism is the production of food stuffs. The family kitchen is the ultimate goal of the result of the best efforts of the united industries of the world. From it comes the life-giving energy which sustains our school children, our industrial workers, our business and professional men, our statesmen. Fathers, sons, daughters are dependent for their comfort and well-being upon a well-ordered, intelligently conducted kitchen.

The chemist who compounds medicine for the sick undergoes a long course of special training before he is allowed to enter the laboratory and perform the important work of preparing medicines. The physician who prescribes the medicine, undergoes a different and even more arduous course of preparation. Would it not be better if the cook who prepares the chemicals by which the life and energy of the family is sustained, replenished or awakened were given some portion of the training bestowed upon these other professions? The physical well being of the well is as important as is that of the sick. The requirements of a body depleted by hard physical or mental labor requires as scientific and hygienic treatment as the invalid's, although more varied and pleasurable.

To arouse and stimulate the appetite that perhaps over-exhaustion, worry or depression has killed, to gratify the healthy, normal appetite without overfeeding and exposing the body to the evils of indigestion through over-rich, ill-assorted or ill-timed dishes, to supply bone and tissue building material to the growing, brain-nourishment to the student and the brain workers, blood-making foods to the aenemics, to forestall the physician and the chemist, is not this a more dignified occupation, a more philanthropic and humane calling than either of those which we are wont to regard as among the foremost professions?

The cook, the housekeeper, should know food and the food value and the peculiar properties of the different viands which she has in her storehouse, just as the chemist knows the medicinal values of the drugs and chemicals in his laboratory. She shuld study the individual needs of her group and arrange her menus to meet them, taking into account the tastes and physical peculiarities of the various members, as well as the time of the meal and the occupations which have preceded the meal or which are to follow it.

While cooking in the home is apparently an unscientific labor and often performed under crude conditions, considering other sciences, it is in reality the oldest of all sciences, reaching back to the very rim of existence of the human family. And since it owes its birth to the elemental, irradicable and avowedly unscientific emotion—love—it is perhaps doubtful if it will ever become an exact science, or be reduced to an exactly scientific basis. However, to every homekeeper nature bequeaths a legacy of intuition, of tradition, of desire, reaching back from her latest ancestress to that early progenitor who first sought to enhance the comfort of her prehistoric family by improving through the labor of love the raw materials which nature afforded for their sustenance.

It may be that we are still too ignorant of the real science of life to determine the value of this "unscientific" element, and to say whether the preparation of food can be put upon a purely so-called scientific basis and brought to perfection by mechanical means. But while time is solving this open question, the facilities are daily increasing whereby the homekeeper may add to that facility and intuition which is the inherited experience of the race, the knowledge which the physician and chemist have gleaned for her benefit as well as their own. A study of the peculiar properties of the various foodstuffs at her command, joined with her knowledge of the characteristics and requirements of those whose welfare she has in her keeping, will suggest to her a course in self-taught chemistry whereby she can prove herself worthy of her long lineage in the gentle art of wise and loving service.

Hints on Eating.

We should eat to live; not live to eat. As a rule we eat too much, too often, too ignorantly. One-fourth of what we eat keeps us, the remaining three-fourths we keep at the risk of our lives. Man is the only animal that will eat when ill.

Appetite is one thing; hunger quite another. Appetite is of the stomach, but hunger is of the mouth. A craving for food is as unnatural as a craving for drink (false stimulants). Both are abnormal. True hunger, as distinguished from appetite, is when the mouth fairly waters at the thought, mention, odor or sight of food.

What to eat? Anything that agrees with you. If you, knowingly, eat or drink anything that does not agree with you, you deserve all the punishment you get. Remember, we are not punished for our physical sins, but by them.

You should get yourself in a perfect condition through exercise and nutritious foods, perfect condition mentally as well as physically (for the mind, through auto-suggestion, plays an important part).

Fear nothing that you eat. If you fear it, do not eat it; if you eat it, do not fear it. Fear is negative and always invites. If you fear dyspepsia, you'll get it. Instead of saying, "I can't eat this and I can't eat that," say instead, "Just show me anything wholesome, anything I like, that I can't eat."

Say good-by to every morsel of food that passes your lips. Say it as if you mean it, not as a Patti farewell, but with a confidence that you will never hear from it again. But, beware, do not let your stomach get it until the first miller, the mouth, is through with it. Also be happy and cheerful as you eat, for a sour countenance causeth a sour stomach.

The drinking of distilled water (or fresh buttermilk) will keep the veins and arteries so supple and free-running that there will be no clogging up, no deposit of irritating and calcareous matter around the joints, nor of poisonous waste in the muscles. It is the stiffeninig and narrowing of the blood vessels which bring on old age. This condition may be postponed anywhere from ten to twenty years by the free use of either distilled water or buttermilk.

Make it a daily rule of your life to drink at least one glass of water when you get up in the morning, and one or two glasses on retiring at night; then work in enough between meals to make up your two quarts per day.

EDWARD B. WARMAN, A. M.

In the general effort toward the betterment of conditions, which characterizes the movements of our times, nothing is more important or more deserving of careful study than the procuring of pure, clean food. The women, homemakers and buyers of food, realize the importance of this element in the physical, mental and spiritual development of those whose welfare is her sacred charge. It is the women who will create public sentiment and public standards which will require makers and sellers of food to comply with the laws. It is the women who will first see the necessity of further regulations to enable them to procure pure, clean food.

The federal and state pure food laws have been enacted for the protection of the people. To arouse a greater interest in a subject which so affects the welfare of our homes and communities, the General Federation and all State Federations of Women's Clubs have created the "pure food committees."

Because "pure food" is a subject so within the realm of every woman's activity, the response to the plan of the National Federation Committee and all State Federation Committees has been so enthusiastic as to merit the name of a national movement on the part of women.

Because of this universal interest in pure food, the National Committee has asked all the women's clubs in the United States to concentrate their efforts upon three very important phases of pure food, to-wit:

First—The study of pure food laws and their enforcement.

Second—The improvement of the milk supply.

Third—The improvement of the sanitary conditions in provision stores.

The study of the pure food law and local conditions is a necessary foundation for this work. The General Federation of Clubs represents a membership of more than 300,000 women. When we realize what a splendid, intelligent force this is, it is not a matter of wonder that all over the United States in the last two years new pure food laws have been enacted in many states and in others old laws have been revised and improved in response to the interest women have shown on the subject of pure food.

The State of Washington has as good a pure food law as any of these United States. It closely follows the federal law and is operated successfully—that is, considering the immense territory and the limited number of deputies which the small funds alloted to this state department will allow.

The 105 Women's Clubs in the State of Washington represent a membership of nearly 4,000 women. Each club will give a part of this year's study to the pure food law and its application to local conditions. While our law is good, there are some things yet to be desired, and some provisions of the law which are not operated so as to get the best results under the law as it now exists. It does not require the spirit of a seer to foresee that when such a number of women give their intelligence and energy to the subject of pure food that we may expect "something doing" in our state.

The present Pure Food Commissioner of Washington is Mr. L. Davies, of Davenport. He will, upon application, send out copies of the "Bulletins of Pure Food" which his office issues for the benefit of the public. The bulletins contain long lists of almost everything to be found on our pantry shelves and tells which are "legal" or "illegal." The distribution of these is one element of the educational work of the Pure Food Committee.

One of the important provisions of our law is that of State Chemist. And Washington is fortunate in having in this capacity Elton Fulmer, who is one of the professors in the State Agricultural College at Pullman. He is a chemist of national reputation, being one of the eight men who constitute "the National Committee of Standards of Purity of Food Products." He is the only member of this committee west of the Mississippi. He is an enthusiast in his work, and has written for the Pure Food Committee articles on the meaning of labels and other phases of the subject, which are of inestimable value as a means of giving to the public technical knowledge which will enable homemakers and merchants alike to buy more intelligently.

Milk, that most important article of diet, especially for the young, has received much intelligent attention from the State and Local Boards of Health. According to recent tests, at least one city in Washington was shown to have a purer milk supply than any other large city in the United States. The dairy conditions over the state are not bad, but "eternal vigilance is the price of pure milk." Complaints of suspicions of dairy conditions should be reported to the local Health Boards or to the State Veterinarian, Dr. S. B. Nelson, Pullman, Washington. Deputies will be sent to make inspections.

Market inspection is an open field for the hygienist and one much in need of intelligent and energetic criticism. Most merchants desire to have their stores in good condition and faults in the case of food are usually matters of oversight and not intentional.

It is a matter of thoughtlessness that leaves calery, for instance exposed to the dirt and germs of a busy street all day to be sent into our homes. Bread distributed about a city in baskets or partly closed wagons cannot, after passing through many hands, be clean when offered to a family at meal time.

Meat and fowls that hang in markets or lie in long rows on a counter, dishes of sausage or buckets of butter and lard that we see uncovered in meat markets, cannot be clean when exposed to the dust and dirt and flies.

Our state pure food law does not specifically provide for

this protection, but the general provision "to procure pure food for man and beast" might be construed to cover these points. In most of the large cities this point has received attention from the Boards of Health. But the Board of Health comprehends such a wide field that all that could be done has not been possible with the limited force.

In some of the cities of Washington a Pure Food Council, consisting of a member from the Board of Health and each Woman's Club, has been formed. The sole object is to all work together to obtain the best conditions which will give pure, clean food and all the blessings which follow in consequence.

This method of procedure is recommended by the Pure Food Committee to every town and city in Washington and has met with hearty response from every quarter.

Why may not Washington have the very best pure food conditions? The members of the Pure Food Committee of the State Federation of Women's Clubs are: Mrs. J. W. Mathews, Pullman; Dr. Sarah Kendall, Seattle; Mrs. E. A. Shores, Tacoma; Mrs. V. A. Marshall, Snohomish; Mrs. A. L. Billings, Lowell.

(Compiled from article by Jennie Wilhite Ellis, Chairman Pure Food Committee, W. S. F. W. C., in Tacoma Ledger.)

Progress of Woman Suffrage.

The friends of equal rights for women will have even a merrier Christmas than usual this year. Those who are fighting in a good cause have always reason to be happy, whether the immediate prospect looks bright or dark; but they have especial cause to rejoice when things are manifestly and visibly coming their way. Let us take a bird's-eye view of the progress of the suffrage movement up to date.

A hundred years ago, women could not vote anywhere, except to a very limited extent in Sweden and a few other places in the old world.

In 1838, Kentucky gave school suffrage to widows with children of school age. In 1850, Ontario gave it to women, both married and single. In 1861, Kansas gave it to all women. In 1867, New South Wales gave women municipal suffrage. In 1869, England gave municipal suffrage to single women and widows; Victoria gave it to women, both married and single, and Wyoming gave full suffrage to all women.

In 1871, West Australia gave municipal suffrage to women. School suffrage was granted in 1875 by Michigan and Minnesota, in 1876 by Colorado, in 1877 by New Zealand, in 1878 by New Hampshire and Oregon, in 1879 by Massachusetts, in 1880 by New York and Vermont.

In 1880, South Australia gave municipal suffrage to women.

In 1881, municipal suffrage was extended to the single women and widows of Scotland, and full parliamentary suffrage in the Isle of Man. Nebraska gave women school suffrage in 1883. Municipal suffrage was given by Ontario and Tasmania in 1884, and by New Zealand and New Brunswick in 1886.

In 1887, municipal suffrage was granted in Kansas, Nova Scotia and Manitoba, and school suffrage in North and South Dakota, Montana, Arizona and New Jersey. In the same year Montana gave tax-paying women the right to vote upon all questions submitted to the taxpayers.

In 1888, England gave women county suffrage, and British Columbia and the Northwest Territory gave them municipal suffrage. In 1889, county suffrage was given to the women of Scotland, and municipal suffrage to single women and widows in the province of Quebec. In 1891, school suffrage was granted in Illinois.

In 1893, school suffrage was granted in Connecticut, and full suffrage in Colorado and New Zealand. In 1894, school suffrage was granted in Ohio, bond suffrage in Iowa, and parish and district suffrage in England to women both married and single. In 1895, full suffrage was granted in South Australia to women both married and single. In 1896, full suffrage was granted in Utah and Idaho.

In 1898, the women of Ireland were given the right to vote for all officers except members of parliament; Minnesota gave women the right to vote for library trustees; Delaware gave school suffrage to tax-paying women; France gave women engaged in commerce the right to vote for judges of the tribunals of commerce, and Louisiana gave tax-paying women the right to vote upon all questions submitted to the taxpayers. In 1900, Wisconsin gave women school suffrage, and West Australia granted full parliamentary suffrage to women both married and single.

In 1901, New York gave tax-paying women in all towns and villages of the state the right to vote on questions of local taxation,, Norway gave them municipal suffrage, and the Kansas Legislature voted down almost unanimously and "amid a ripple of amusement" a proposal to repeal municipal suffrage.

In 1902, full national suffrage was granted to all the women of federated Australia, and state suffrage to the women of New South Wales.

In 1903, full suffrage was granted to the women of Tasmania, and bond suffrage to the women of Kansas.

In 1905, Queensland gave women full suffrage. In 1906, Finland gave full national suffrage to women and made them eligible to all offices, from members of parliament down.

In 1907, Norway gave full parliamentary suffrage to the 300,000 women who already had municipal suffrage, Sweden made women eligible to municipal office, Denmark gave women the right to vote for members of boards of public charities, and to serve on such boards; Russia gave women of property a proxy vote in the election of members of the douma, England made them eligible as mayors, aldermen and county and town councillors, and Finland elected nineteen women to parliament. In 1908, Denmark gave municipal suffrage to all women who are taxpayers or the wives of taxpayers; Michigan gave tax-paying women the right to vote on questions of local taxation, and Finland elected twenty-five women to parliament.

Political sagacity has been defined as the power to tell a band wagon from a hearse.—A. S. B., in The Woman's Journal.

How Washington Women Lost the Ballot

(By Adella M. Parker.)

How the women of Washington lost the ballot, though the men twice voted it to them; how Tacoma's "boss" gambler attacked the law to get "his man" out of the "pen"; how a bartender's wife rushed a case through the courts and refused to let it go higher; how, in '89, the ballots were "marked" before they came from the press—this is the story of how Washington women were tricked out of their political rights.

Women first voted in Washington in 1884. They were enfranchised by the legislature of the previous year. They voted during '85 and '86, and they voted so well that they drove most of the thugs and gamblers over into British Columbia, and the British themselves were forced to enfranchise women "in self-protection," as was stated by the honorable member who brought in the bill.

The women of British Columbia still have the ballot. There are no courts on the British side to question acts of parliament. But in Washington, though the suffrage laws have never been repealed, woman's right to vote was denied by the courts in '87, the power of the legislature to give her the right to vote was denied in '88, and in '89 she was counted out by a ballot "marked" in the printing.

Harry Morgan, "boss" gambler of Tacoma, made the first attack upon the suffrage laws. It was he who was back of the famous case of Harland vs. Territory (3 W. T.), which first denied the women the right to vote. Harland was a henchman of Morgan who had been convicted on a felony charge and sent to prison. Both men and women sat on the jury which brought in the verdict, and Morgan challenged the right of women to act as jurors.

The right of women to serve on the jury depended upon their right to vote. For three years they had been voting, unchallenged, and they had been serving as jurors with such marked ability as to call forth the most favorable comment for their capacity to enforce the law.

But woman's capacity in this respect did not recommend her to Harry Morgan, and he was determined to drive her from the courtroom. Defeated in Harland vs. Territory in the lower court, he appealed to the higher.

And he won. Harland vs. Territory was decided in favor of Harland. Judge George Turner wrote the opinion, holding that women had no right to sit on the jury because the law granting them the privilege was not given the proper title.

The title of the bill was "An act to amend Section 3050 of Chapter 238 of the Code of Washington." Nineteen other laws passed by the same legislature had been headed in the same way and the very bill authorizing the sitting of the court which pronounced this decision was one of them. Yet, though nothing was urged against these other laws, the suffrage law was declared void.

This decision was made by a divided court. Chief Justice Roger S. Greene and Judge John P. Hoyt both held the suffrage law to be valid. But Judge Hoyt was disqualified from sitting in the case because he had been the trial judge in the lower court. Had he been qualified to act the validity of the law would have been sustained, but, as it was, it was possible for two men—Justices George Turner and William Langford, both appointees of Grover Cleveland (peace to his ashes!)—to deprive all the women in Washington of the ballot on a mere technicality which was not urged against scores of other laws and one which was later overthrown by a unanimous court; for this ruling was completely reversed in Marston vs. Humes (3 Wash.) four years later. Judge Hoyt, with the full bench concurring, delivered the opinion of the court, and after making an exhaustive survey of the cases, cited in support of the decision in Harland vs. Territory, he makes the comment that if the learned judges who made that decision had read the cases which they cited they would have decided the case the other way. He excuses them on the ground that there were few books in the territory and that digests are often misleading.

But Harland vs. Territory did not finally take away from Washington women the right to vote. This case was decided in February, 1887. The legislature which met the following winter had already been chosen by the votes of both men and women; and during that session a new suffrage law was passed, having a sufficient title to bring it within the ruling of the court.

This law was passed early in 1888. In April of that year women voted at the spring elections, but in Spokane one woman's vote was challenged, while the votes of all the others were accepted by the election officials.

The vote of Mrs. Nevada Bloomer was refused. Mrs. Nevada Bloomer was a bartender's wife, and she at once brought an action for $5,000 damages against Todd and other election officers for the injury she sustained by being deprived of her vote.

On April 9, 1888, George Turner resigned from the Supreme Bench and became an attorney in this suit, defending the election officials.

The case of Bloomer vs. Todd (3 W. T.) was rushed through the courts at a lively rate. Though the Supreme Court was a year behind its docket, this case was advanced on the calendar and decided in four months. Four of the five judges then making up the court concurred in the view that Mrs. Nevada Bloomer had suffered no injury because she had no right to vote.

Chief Justice Jones wrote this opinion, which followed Judge Turner's brief. The territorial legislature had failed to give Mrs. Navada Bloomer the right to vote, not because it had meant to withhold the right or had wished to do so. The legislature had passed a suffrage law and there was this time no defect in its title. But the legislature hadn't given Mrs. Nevada Bloomer the right to vote because it couldn't.

In this decision the court did not assume that Congress had no right to authorize the territory to enfranchise women, nor does it claim that the organic act under which the territory was organized expressly excludes women from the ballot. In fact, the court admits that Congress does authorize the territory to enfranchise "citizens," barring the criminal and the insane, and the court will not, of course, claim that woman is not a citizen; but, the court, following closely still the brief of the Hon. George Turner, did find that Congress should have put the word "male" before the word citizen in the organic act, and inasmuch as Congress did not put it in, but, in fact, left it out, the court took the liberty to amend this act of Congress by inserting it.

The amended act now read that the territory could enfranchise only "male" citizens, and, of course, this barred Mrs. Nevada Bloomer.

Now, at this time the women of Wyoming Territory had been voting for twenty years, and in Utah also women were voting, and in at least two cases Utah women had taken to the United States Supreme Court questions similar to that involved in this action and had won them. So, willing friends at once came to the aid of Mrs. Bloomer. Funds were placed at her disposal. That $5,000 might still be hers if she would carry the case to the United States Court. But Mrs. Nevada Bloomer refused. She was perhaps convinced that she had no right to vote, for nothing could induce her to pursue that $5,000, even with all her expenses paid.

Bloomer vs. Todd was decided in August, 1888. When the statehood bill was rushed through the next winter the reason for the haste was plain. Women were to be excluded from voting for members of the constitutional convention, and suffrage was to be left out of the new state government. As four-fifths of the women were voting at the previous elections, no other method could have been successful in accomplishing this result.

Members of the constitutional convention were to be elected in May. Had Mrs. Bloomer consented to carry the case up, the federal question involved might have been decided before this time. To start a new action and reach a decision within this time was impossible, and any other course might delay statehood. The women were begged not to do this, and all were eager for admission to the Union.

Furthermore, the women were assured that if they would trust to the chivalry of the men suffrage would be incorporated into the new constitution.

So the women trusted to the chivalry of the men, and when the constitutional convention met two of the seventy-five members were in favor of suffrage for women. This is the statement of Henry C. Blackwell, who canvassed it thoroughly.

Neither woman suffrage nor prohibition was inserted in the constitution, but they were presented as separate amendments at the same election. Considering the make-up of the convention, this may seem a remarkable concession, but in the light of later events but little risk of enacting them into law appears to have been run.

The prohibitionists at the fall election had not put any

ticket in the field, with the understanding that the republicans had printed a ballot marked in advance, voting down the amendments, and had even printed it on the prohibition printing press.

There are men in Seattle who know just how this trick was turned. It was generally believed at the time that agents of a large wholesale liquor house not having its headquarters in Portland, had offered to print all the republican ballots for the whole state without cost to the party if allowed this privilege. (There was no Australian ballot system in the territory. Each party got out its ballots and gave them out at the polls.)

These facts are known. The small printing office of the Leader—the prohibition paper—at Third and Wall streets. in Seattle, was hired for forty-eight hours, under lock and key, to print the republican ballots. No one in the Leader office was employed on the work. Printers were brought from elsewhere, the work was done and the office had been thoroughly cleaned up when the Leader staff regained possession.

In cleaning up the press a crumpled ballot was found shoved down behind it. This was the first intimation of any irregularity. A member of the republican committee was confronted with it. He claimed that only 2,000 or 3,000 of these fraudulent ballots had been printed—"vest pocket" votes for the liquor interests. He finally admitted that there were 60,000 or 70,000, but the press registered 180,000.

It was three days before election. The prohibitionists sent out 125 telegrams, "Watch for fraudulent republican votes." Many points, of course, could not be reached. Large numbers of the ballots were returned to headquarters and clean ones demanded or none. But thousands of these marked ballots were given out on election day, and, in spite of challenges, thousands were voted and counted. The amendments were lost, but a change of one vote in twelve would have carried them.

WASHINGTON WOMEN'S COOK BOOK.

Election October 1st, 1889.

For Representative to 51st Congress
  JOHN L. WILSON
For Governor
  ELISHA P FERRY
For Lieutenant Governor
  CHARLES E. LAUGHTON.
For Secretary of State
  ALLEN WEIR
For State Treasurer
  ADDISON A LINDSLEY
For State Auditor.
  THOMAS M REED
For Attorney General:
  WILLIAM C. JONES.
For Superintendent of Public Instruction:
  ROBERT B. BRYAN
For Commissioner of Public Lands
  WILLIAM T FORREST
For Judges of the Supreme Court
  RALPH O DUNBAR,
  THEODORE L STILES,
  JOHN P HOYT,
  THOMAS J. ANDERS,
  ELMON SCOTT

FIRST—For the Constitution
  Against the Constitution.
SECOND—For Woman-Suffrage.
  Against Woman Suffrage.
THIRD—For Prohibition.
  Against Prohibition
FOURTH—For the Permanent Location of the Seat of Government

King County Republican Ticket.

For Judge of the Superior Court,
  JULIUS A STRATTON
For County Clerk,
  M M HOLMES

Legislative Ticket.

For State Senators 19th Senatorial District,
  W D WOOD,
  J H JONES,
  O D GUILFOIL,
  J R KINNEAR,
  W V RINEHART.
For Representatives King County,
  J. T BLACKBURN,
  W C RUTTER,
  W. H HUGHES,
  ALEXANDER ALLEN
  W. J. SHINN,
  GEO. BOTHELL,
  F. W BIRD,
  FRED J GRANT.

Some Legal Opinions

All citizens 21 years old, and not convicted of any crime which would deprive them of the legal right to vote, should have equal privileges under the law.—William G. Cochran, Sullivan, Ill., Circuit Judge Sixth District.

Women cannot be safe until they have the ballot; men cannot be safe until women have it. The State needs everyone's contribution of thought and action—women's as well as men's—and that now needs women's a little the most.—Henry D. Lloyd, Chicago.

Ballot restrictions should not be drawn at the line of sex. In the social economy the responsibilities of woman are no less important than those of man, and these responsibilities she assumes and bears with splendid honor and credit to her sex.

I am a devout believer in "equal rights for all and special privileges to none." Democracy has thoroughly exploded the long-time myth of the inequality of woman. I am persuaded there can be advanced no sound reason, morally or intellectually, against her political emancipation.—Walter I. Manny, State's Attorney Brown County, State's Attorneys' Association of Illinois.

That only is a true republic in which every mature, moral and intelligent human being is allowed to vote.—Thomas Taylor, Jr., Master-in-Chancery, Lakeside, Ill.

The laws of Illinois for and in aid of good morals will be better and more surely enforced when the women have the same rights with men in selecting officers to enforce such laws. I always have been in favor of their right to vote."—W. Scott Edwards, County Judge Fulton County.

"Women's rights under the law should equal her responsibilities before the law."—David S. Geer, Chicago.

With unrestricted male suffrage, I am inclined to believe we should have unrestricted female suffrage. It would, in my opinion, largely neutralize the evil effects of unrestricted male suffrage.—William J. Franklin, County Judge McDonough County, Illinois.

An unrestricted suffrage is dangerous in proportion to the moral tone of those who exercise it. To raise the moral tone safeguards the suffrage pro tanto. To extend the suffrage to women will raise the moral tone. While the country would be benefited by a restricted suffrage, such restriction should apply without regard to sex.—Henry C. Ward, County Judge Whiteside County, Illinois.

I deem it a disgrace to allow the negro and the Dagoes to vote and make our American ladies stand back. Suffrage is not a question of sex, but of moral fitness. Our women bear their share of the government's burdens and are not allowed representation. It is wrong.—Charles B. Thomas, County Judge Hamilton County, Illinois.

Taxation without representation is unpopular from our earliest history. Equal rights to all and special privileges to none will never cease to be a popular sentiment in the American heart. I am in favor of the women of this country having a voice in the making and the executing of the laws in which they are equally interested with men. The proper exercise of the elective franchise and the purity of the ballot is most essential for our country's welfare. The women of the land surely have an equal interest with men in the country's weal or woe. Give them the ballot and they will use it for the country's best good.—P. W. Gallagher, Judge of City Court of Canton, Ill.

I have always been in favor of the equality of men and women before the law, including full suffrage for women. I presided at the birth of the American Woman Suffrage Association at Cleveland in 1869.—James B. Bradwell, former County Judge, Editor Chicago Legal News.

Believing in equal rights for all, I am in favor of extending the right of suffrage to women upon the same conditions that it is granted to men. The suffrage ought to include everyone capable of properly and intelligently exercising the right.—James H. Cartwright, Judge Supreme Court of Illinois.

I favor full suffrage for women.

1. It will enable them to better protect their persons and their property.

2. It will tend to purify politics.

3. Because men and women can govern better conjointly than either can separately.

4. Because women have as much right to the ballot as men, and it is only a matter of justice to give it to them.

The accident of sex should make no difference in human

rights.—Murray F. Tuley, Chicago, Circuit Judge Cook County.

If the women of this State desire the right to vote it should be accorded to them. The question is not whether thus the people of the State would be better governed. For under the principles and traditions of American liberty, men and women, too, are entitled, not merely to a good government, but to self-government. Any possible deterioration in this regard, which I should not, however, anticipate, would be more than compensated by the indication of this great underlying principle of American constitutional liberty.—S. S. Gregory, Chicago.

There never was an argument advanced against woman suffrage which would not equally apply to teaching women the alphabet.—Edward Osgood Brown, Chicago, Circuit Judge Cook County.

ADDITIONAL RECIPES.

Banana Chutney

1 cup ~~sugar~~ Slice dry bananas thin & mix with a pound of finely cut Spanish onion & one half a pound of chopped dates — Pour over 1½ cups best vinegar, boil until tender. Mash fine. Then add ¼ lb crystallized ginger cut fine, 1 teaspoonful curry powder, 1 teasp salt — ½ lb syrup. Boil again — Seal while hot —

California Chutney

1 cup uncooked prunes —
1½ cups vinegar
2 cups brown sugar
1 tblsp dry mustard
½ teasp cinnamon
½ teasp salt — ½ teasp cayenne
2 cups chopped apples —
1 cup seedless raisins — 1 cup chopped onion — 1 cup canned or fresh tomatoes

ADDITIONAL RECIPES.

Directions — Banana Chutney — (preceding page) —

California Chutney —

Boil prunes ten minutes, then remove pits & chop — Combine vinegar with sugar, mustard, ginger, onion, salt & cayenne. when it boils, add apples, prunes, raisins, onions & tomatoes. Continue boiling until mixture is desired consistency, about 30 minutes, stirring often to prevent burning — Pour into sterilized jars & seal while hot —

ADDITIONAL RECIPES.

Dr. Mayo's Recipe for Rheumatism — (Laxative.)
1 qt of cold water
Juice of three lemons
1 Tablespoonful Baking Soda
(Ditto) Cream of Tartar & Epsom Sa
Shake — a glass three or four times
daily.

ADDITIONAL RECIPES

Grapefruit Meringue Half Shells —
2 g.f., 1/4 cup sugar*, whites 2 eggs —
1/4 cup coconut. Fold g.f. pieces into meringue
sprinkle with coconut — top with g.f. pieces
Brown in slow oven (300°) about 20 min.
(* add gradually) Serve hot or cold

Cranberry O. Relish in Shells
4 cups (1 lb.) cranberries
2 unpeeled oranges — 2 cups sugar —
Put o. & c. thro' grinder — mix sugar — & let
stand a few hrs. serve in shells —
garnish (for meats)

Carotene Salad —
1 1/2 cups o. pieces   1/2 cup raisins
1 1/2 " finely cut carrot — 1/2 cup peanuts
any kind dressing
garnish with raisins

All Season Salad —
1 cup or. pieces. 2 cups diced apples
1/2 cup diced celery — 1/2 cup walnuts
In lettuce cups — mayonaise made with
sunkist lemon juice —

O. & L. juice Cocktail
3 c. charged water or ginger ale
1/2 cup sugar, 1 cup o. juice
a few gr. of salt — 1/2 " lemon juice
pour over cracked ice in cocktail glasses
garnish sprigs of mint or maraschino cherries —

ADDITIONAL RECIPES.

Orange Marshmallow Dessert —
1 1/2 cups orange juice
1/2 lb (32) marshmallows
1 tbsp. lemon juice
O. sections (2 O.) Melt in double boiler
Pour over O sections — chill til stiff —
(Serves four)

Club Fruit Plate —
Lettuce cup. cottage cheese — melon
or avocado balls — banana finger,
orange slices, balls of cream cheese,
walnut halves — any dressing — *
arrange according to taste —
balls of cream cheese — walnut halves

ADDITIONAL RECIPES.

ADDITIONAL RECIPES.

ADDITIONAL RECIPES.

ADDITIONAL RECIPES.

ADDITIONAL RECIPES.

ADDITIONAL RECIPES.

ADDITIONAL RECIPES.

ADDITIONAL RECIPES.

ADDITIONAL RECIPES.

ADDITIONAL RECIPES.

ADDITIONAL RECIPES.

ADDITIONAL RECIPES.

ADDITIONAL RECIPES.

ADDITIONAL RECIPES.

ADDITIONAL RECIPES.

ADDITIONAL RECIPES.

ADDITIONAL RECIPES.

ADDITIONAL RECIPES.

ADDITIONAL RECIPES:

ADDITIONAL RECIPES.

ADDITIONAL RECIPES.

ADDITIONAL RECIPES.

ADDITIONAL RECIPES.

ADDITIONAL RECIPES.

ADDITIONAL RECIPES.

ADDITIONAL RECIPES.

ADDITIONAL RECIPES.

ADDITIONAL RECIPES.

ADDITIONAL RECIPES.

ADDITIONAL RECIPES.

INDEX

Beverages— Page.
How to Make Good Coffee. 125
Good Tea 125
How to Make Good Tea...125
A Cup of Excellent Chocolate 126
Fruit Punch 126
Fruit Eggnog 126

Beauty and Hygiene, Hints for—
Cucumber Cream 190
For Rough and Cracked Skin 190
To Whiten Complexion....190
Nail Plaste 190
Hand Lotion 191
To Keep Hands Free from Stain 191
Hair Remover 191
Cold Cream 191
Nail Powder 191
For Red Hands 191
Tooth Wash 191
Toilet Water 192
Carnation Toilet Water....192
Menthol Vinegar for Headache Cologne...........192
Lotion for Bunions.......192
Powder for the Feet......192
Good Shampoo 192
Cold Cream 192
Hints on Breathing........193
Hints on Bathing.........193
Health Exercise 193
What to Do on Arising....194
Hints on Eating..........197

Bread—
Bread 53
Yeast 53
Yeast No. 2............... 53
Bread 53
Unleavened Parker House Rolls 54
Cream Biscuit 54
Sally Lunns 54
Tea Biscuit 54
Graham Gems 54
Brown Bread 54
Graham Bread with Raisins 55
Graham Drop Cakes....... 55

Page.
Graham Muffins 55
Waffles 55
Waffles No. 2............. 55
Waffles No. 3............. 56
Potato Pancakes 56
Pancakes 56
Lemon Crackers 56
Sally Lunns 56
Biscuit 56
Sour Milk Biscuit......... 56
Beaten Biscuit 57
Parker House Rolls....... 57
Corn or "Johnny" Cakes.. 57
Steamed Brown Bread..... 57
Brown Bread 57
Pop-Overs 58
Quick Nut Bread......... 58
Nut Rolls 58
Bread 58
Whole Wheat Bread....... 59
"Mrs. Wardall's Prison Fare" 59
Rice Corn Bread......... 59
Tender Graham Gems..... 59

Breakfast and Luncheon—
Toast 47
French Toast 47
Fried Rolls 47
Eggs; Soft Boiled 47
Plain Omelet 48
Scrambled Eggs 48
Stuffed Eggs 48
Eggs Poached in Milk..... 48
Shirred Eggs 48
A Breakfast Dish......... 49
Scalloped Potatoes 49
Potato Balls 49
Luncheon Relish 49
Breakfast Potatoes 49
Creamed Codfish 49
Dutch Pon-Hoss 50
Sausage 50

Cakes—
Chocolate Frosting 83
Frosting 83
Dry Frosting 83
Boiled Icing 83
Chocolate Icing 83
Chocolate Filling 84

INDEX---Continued

	Page.
Caramel Filling	84
Caramel Filling No. 2	84
Prize Fruit Cake	84
Wedding Cake	85
Mahogany Cake	85
Filling	85
Tilden Cake-Loaf Cake	85
Devil's Food Cake	86
Marble Cake	86
Potato Cake	86
The Famous Lady Baltimore Cake	86
Devil's Food	87
Silver Cake	87
Gold Cake	87
Silver Cake	87
Gold Cake	88
Tea Cakes	88
Walnut Cake	88
Caramel Cake	88
Potato Caramel Cake	88
Prune Cake	89
Sunshine Cake	89
Pork Cake	89
Cream Cake	89
Apple Sauce Cake	90
Chocolate Cake	90
Roll Jelly Cake	90
White Cake	90
Sponge Cake	90
Hot Water Sponge Cake	91
Layer Cake	91
White Perfection Cake	91
Fruit Cake	91
Rolled Jelly Cake	91
Pecan Nut Cake	92
Coffee Cake	92
Layer Cake	92
Molasses Layer Cake	92
Eggless Cake	92
Apple Fruit Cake	93
Dutch Apple Cake	93
Rocks	93
Marguerites	93
Doughnuts	94
Cookies No. 1	94
Cookies No. 2	94
Oatmeal Cakes	94
Oatmeal Crisps (Excellent)	94
Hermits	94
Apple Rolls	95

	Page.
Snowball Doughnuts	95
Michigan Doughnuts	95
Cream Puffs	95
Cookies	95
Rolled Oats Cookies	96
Rocks	96
Brownies	96
Caraway Cookies	96
Never-Fail Ginger Bread	96
Peanut Cookies	96
Belgian Hare Ginger Bread	97
Egg Bakkelse, Egg Cookies	97
Fattigman Cookies	97
Sand Bakkelse—Sand Cookies	97
Ginger Cookies	98
Rice Cakes	98
Cheese Rice	98
Rice Cakes	98
Rice Croquettes	98
Fruit Cake	98
Golden Dressing	99
Black Pudding	99
Fruit Mince for Pies	99

Canning, Preserves, Pickles, Etc.

	Page.
Canned Peaches	108
Canned Strawberries	108
Baked Prunes	108
Baked Pears	109
Baked Apples	109
Baked Apples No. 2	109
Jellies	109
Currant Jelly	110
Apple Jelly	110
Crab Apple Jelly	110
Currants in Jell	110
Fruit Juice	111
Canned Raspberries	111
Rhubarb Marmalade, Scotch Recipe	111
Orange Marmalade	111
Orange Marmalade, No. 2	111
Spiced Cherries	112
Chow Chow	112
Tomato Catsup	112
Oil Pickles	113
Mustard Pickles	113
Variety Pickles	113
German Mustard	113
Chile Sauce	114

INDEX---Continued

	Page.
Piccalilli	114
Green Tomato Pickles	114
Beet Pickle Chow-Chow	114
Nutmeg Melon Pickles	114
Quick Pickles	115
Sweet Pickled Peaches	115
Spiced Jelly	115
Mint Jelly	115
Carve, How to	181

Cheese Dishes—

Welsh Rarebit	45
Never-Fail Welsh Rarebit (for 12 persons)	45
Cheese Straws	45
Cheese Fondu	45
Cheese Canaps	46
Cheese Salad	46
Cheese Balls	46
Cheese Omelet	46

Clams—

Steamed Clams	17
Baked Clams	17
Clam Puree	17
Clams on Toast	18
Fried Clams	18
Clam Croquettes	18
Scrambled Clams with Eggs	18
Pan Roast a la Doane	18
Clam Fritters	18
Clam Pie	18
Clam Omelet	19
Scalloped Clams	19

Confectionery—

Nut Candy	116
Cocoanut Kisses	116
Cream Walnuts	116
Fudges	117
Sea Foam	117
Caramels	117
Nut Candy	117
White Taffy	117
Molasses Candy	118
Marshmallows	118
Penouche	118
Seafoam	118
Turkish Delight	119
Nougat	119
Divinity	119
Fudge	120

	Page.
Fudge No. 2	120
Taffy	120
Marshmallows	120
Christmas Candy	120
Peanut Candy	121
Burnt Sugar Candy	121
Butter Scotch	121
Chocolate Caramels	122
Stuffed Dates	122

Desserts, Pudding Sauces—

Lemon Sauce	60
Milk Sauce	60
Egg Sauce	60
Strawberry Sauce	60
Hard Sauce	60
English Plum Pudding	61
Plum Pudding	61
Steamed Pudding	61
Panama Cream	61
Orange Marmalade Pudding	62
Puff Pudding	62
Browned Rice and Raisins	62
Mysterious Pudding	62
Rice Pudding	62
Cranberry Pudding	63
Date Pudding	63
Apple Dumpling	63
Apple Fritters	63
Strawberry Dumplings	64
Sago Pudding	64
Corn Pudding	64
Baked Apples	64
Prune Whip	64
Orange Pudding	65
Steamed Bread Pudding	65
Cornstarch Pudding	65
Steamed Carrot Pudding	65
Tapioca Pudding	66
Custard Pudding	66
Rice Custard	66
Mountain Dew	66
Caramel Custard	67
Custard Pudding	67
Chess Cake or Transparent Custard	67
Blackberry Pudding	67
Fruit Gelatine	67
Blackberry Pandowdy	68
Banana Whip	68
Marshmallow Gelatine	68

INDEX---Continued

	Page.
Almond Parfait	68
Pineapple Charlotte	68
Fruit Cocktail	69
Ambrosia	69
Fruit Juice Jelly	69
Orange Gelatine	69
Mock Cantaloupe	70
Marshmallow Cream	70
Banana Charlotte	70
Velvet Cream	70
Strawberries in Cream	70
Peach Dessert	71
Spanish Cream	71
Raspberry Cream	71
Strawberry Parfait	72
Muskmelons with Ice Cream	72
Luncheon Parfait	72
Strawberry Mousse	72
Cranberry Bavarian Cream	72
Strawberry Float	73
Banana Custard	73
Fruit Tapioca Pudding	73
Christmas Sherbet	73
Strawberry Sherbet	74
Cranberry Sherbet	74
Fruit Sherbet	74
Grape Sherbet	74
Frozen Cherries	75
Strawberry and Lemon Ice	75
Mixed Fruit Sherbet	75
Ginger Water Ice	75

Entrees—

Sauce for Croquettes	28
Veal Croquettes	28
Chicken Cutlets	28
Aspic Jelly	28
Chicken Croquettes	29
Scalloped Chicken	29
Spanish Meat Balls	29
Spaghetti a la Italienne	29
Creamed Salmon	30
Fish au Gratin	30
Scalloped Sweet Corn	30
Cheese Custard	30
Salmon Pudding	30
Shrimp Pudding	31
Asparagus Entree	31
Timbales Regence, Mushroom Sauce	31
Fried Bananas	31

	Page.
Fried Apples	32
Spanish Rice	32

Fish and Shell Fish—

Clam Chowder	13
Excellent Clam Soup	13
Clam Chowder	13
Clam Fritters	14
Clam Boullion	14
Creamed Clams	14
Clam Fritters	14
Scalloped Oysters	14
Oyster Cocktails	15
Oyster Cocktails	15
Oyster Omelet	15
Ludt Fish	15
Baked Salmon	15
Baked Salmon Spanish	16
Fried Smelts	16
Boiled Fish	16
Fish Turbot	16

FOOD FOR THE SICK.

Liquids—

Chicken Broth	154
Mutton Broth	155
Beef Tea	155
Beef Juice	155
Bullion	155
Flaxseed Tea	155
Barley Water	155
Cornmeal Gruel	156
Flour Gruel	156
Arrowroot Gruel	156
Koumyss	156
Albumen Water	156
Egg and Orange Juice	156
Eggnog	156
Cocoa	157
Tea	157
Coffee	157

Soup—

Cream of Potato	157
Tomato Bisque	157
Cream of Celery	157

Eggs—

Boiled for Typhoid Patients	158
Shirred Egg	158

INDEX---Continued

	Page.
Steamed Egg	158
Omelet	158
Bronilli	158

Oysters—
Pan Roast	158
Pan Broil	158
Creamed Oysters	159
Baked in Shells	159
Macaroni and Oysters	159
Oysters and Celery	159
Oyster Poulette	159

Chicken—
Chicken Jelly	160
Chicken Bondins	160
Creamed Chicken	160
Pressed Chicken	160

Meat—
Raw Beef Sandwich	160
Scrapped Beef	160
Steak	160
Chop	160
Bird	160
Bacon	160

Vegetables—
Spinach	161
Creamed Celery	161
Stuffed Potato	161
Rice	161

Desserts—
Junket	161
Blanc Mange Souffle	162
Sauce for Souffle	162
Baked Custard	162
Orange Cream	162
Farina Jelly	162
Tapioca Cream	163
Snow Pudding	163
Custard Sauce	163
Orange Pudding	163
Baked Bananas	163

German Cooking—
Sauer Braten	170
Bismarck's Favorite	170
Wiener Schnitzel (Veal Cutlets)	171
Kraut Wickel (Cabbage Wraps)	171
Cabbage with Mutton	171
Blitz Cohn, Lightning Cake	171
S. Cookies	172
Cookies	172
Hazelnut Macaroons	172
Prune Pie	172
Zimmersteres (Cinnamon Stars)	172
Pie Crust	173
Lemon Ice	173
Pudding Sauce	173
Apple Pie	173
German Cookies	173
German Pancakes	173

Household Department—
To Boil Water Without Burning	186
Hard Soap for Laundry and Kitchen	186
Cleaning and Laundry	186
Sweeping	187
Making and Applying Wood Stains	187

How Washington Lost the Ballot— 204

Household Economy and Helpful Hints—
A Bit of Economy	164
To Fry Old Fowl That It May Taste Like Spring Chicken	164
To Make Two Pounds of Butter Out of One	164
To Preserve Bread Crumbs	165
Maple Syrup	165
Stale Bread Hot Cakes	165
Peanut Butter	165
To Fry Eggs	166
The Holy Stove	167
Fireless Cooker	168
Kitchen Measures	169

Ices and Sherbets—
Philadelphia Ice Cream	105
Neapolitan Ice Cream	105
Strawberry and Pineapple Ice Cream	105
Pineapple Ice Cream	105
Lemon Sherbet	106
Orange Sherbet	106
Pineapple Sherbet	106

INDEX---Continued

	Page.
A Good Fruit Ice	106
Combination Sherbet	106
Pineapple Sherbet	106

Meats—
Roast Beef	20
Fillet Roast of Beef	20
Flank Steak	20
Favorite Roast Turkey	20
Sheep's Tongue Spanish	21
Veal Loaf	21
Cabbage Rolls	21
Beef Loaf	21
Baked Liver	22
Veal Cutlets	22
Boneless Birds	22
Veal Stew	22
Fried Chicken	23
Chicken with Baked Dumplings	23
Smothered Chicken	23
Luncheon Chicken	23
Chicken Pie	24
Baked Chicken (Southern Style)	24
Boiled Leg of Lamb, Caper Sauce	24
Veal Stew	24
Dumplings for Meat	24
Picnic Meat	25
Oyster Chestnut Dressing (for fowl)	25
Dressing for Fowl or Meat	25

Meat and Fish Sauce—
Tartar Sauce	26
Cream Sauce	26
Fish Sauce	26
Tomato Sauce (for Boiled Tongue)	26
Mushroom Sauce	27
Fried Egg Plant	27
Carrots and Green Peas	27
Summer Squash	27

Menus—
A Christmas Dinner	100
A Washington State Dinner	100
Menu for an Informal Summer Luncheon	101
Menu for an Informal Winter Luncheon	103

	Page.

Miscellaneous—
Chestnut Cream Soup	174
Puree of Sweet Potatoes	174
Spiced Beef Appetizer	174
Tomatoes Stuffed with Succotash	174
Mayonnaise Dressing	174
Mrs. Thompson's Johnny Cake	175
Brown Bread	175
Mrs. Kendall's Johnny Cake	175
Rolled Oats Rolls	175
Billie's Brown Bread	176
Mayonnaise Dressing	176
Cheese Fondue	176
Fruit and Vegetable Salad	177
Fruit and Nut Salad	177
Fruit and Nut Salad	177
Spanish or Mexican Beans	177
Baked Potatoes	177
Potato Peanuts	177
Pepper Cups	178
Sandwich Fillings	178
Salmon Loaf with Rice	178
Salmon Loaf Steamed	179
Hungarian Stew for Five Persons	179
Pressed Meat	179
Summer Mince Meat	180
To Crack Pecans	180
Pineapples, How to Cut	180
Chestnut Cakes	180
Chestnut Glace	180

Mountaineer's Chapter—
How to Build a Camp Fire	127
Provisions for Four People One Week	128
List of Kitchen Outfit	128
Mountaineer's Recipes for Four Persons	129
Tea	129
Coffee	129
Cocoa	129
Baking Powder Bread	130
Biscuit	130
Corn Bread	130
Carr's Yeast Bread	137
Macaroni with Cheese	131
Macaroni with Tomatoes	131

INDEX---Continued

	Page.
Bannocks or Open-Fire Bread	131
Griddle Cakes	131
Boiled Rice	132
Oatmeal Mush	132
Cornmeal Mush	132
Boiled Beans	132
Baked Beans	132
Bean Soup	133
Prospector's Soup	133
Erbswurst Soup	133
Rice Tomato Soup	133
Pearl Barley Soup	134
Creamed Codfish and Potatoes	134
White Sauce	134
To Cook Trout in the Forest	134
To Fry Venison in Camp	135
Venison Chops — Hunter's Style	135
Spanish Sauce for Meats	135
Roast Meat	135
Bacon and Ham	136
Boiled Ham	136
Chipped Beef in Cream	136
Overland Trout	136
Stewed Fruits	136
Carr's Hardtack Pudding	136
Carr's Fruit Cake	137
Cornstarch Pudding	137
Ginger Cake	137
Mince Meat	137
Dough Gods	138

Men's List of Absolute Necessities—

Man Pack Trip	138
Men's Personal Outfit for One Month's Outing—Pack Horse Trip	139
Women's List for the Mountains	139

Progress of Woman Suffrage 201

Pastry—

English Mince Meat	79
Rhubarb Pie	79
Cream Lemon Pie	79
Lemon Pie	79
Pumpkin Pie	79
Blackberry Pie	80

	Page
Apple Pie	80
Cocoanut Custard Pie	80
Custard Pie	80
Lemon Pie—Reliable	81
Cream Pie	81
Banana Pie	81
Vinegar Pie	81
Mock Cherry Pie	81
Squash Pie	82
Ripe Custard Pie	82

Pineapple Desserts—

Pineapple Sponge	76
Pineapple Float	76
Pineapple Parfait	76
Pineapple Souffle	76
Pineapple Delight	76
Pineapple and Strawberry Dessert	77
Turkish Pineapple Cream	77
Gooseberry Pudding	77
Strawberry Sponge Roll	77

Salads—

Never-fail Mayonaise Dressing	33
Cooked Salad Dressing	33
Steamed Mayonaise	33
Salad Dressing	34
Salad Dressing That Will Keep Six Months	34
Sour Cream Dressing	34
Potato Salad Dressing	34
Chicken and Nut Salad	34
Chicken Salad	35
Lobster Salad	35
Potato Salad	35
Potato Salad No. 2	35
Fruit Salad	36
Emergency Salad	36
Tomato Jelly Salad	36
Grape Salad	36
Cherry Salad	36
Stuffed Tomato Salad	36
Cabbage Salad (Quickly Made)	36
Apple Salad	37
Bean Potato Salad	37
Hot Slaw	37
Novel Beet Salad	37
Washington or A.-Y.-P. Fruit Salad	33

INDEX---Continued

	Page		Page
Grape Fruit Salad	38	Cheese Sandwiches	51
Fruit Salad	38	Sandwich Dressing	51
Luncheon Salad	38	Ham Sandwiches	51
Waldorf Salad	38	Club Sandwiches	52
Peach Salad	39	Lettuce Sandwiches	52
Carrot Salad	39	Cheese Sandwiches	52
My Potato Salad	39		
Mayonaise Dressing, with Pure Olive Oil	39	Science in the Kitchen—	195
		Some Legal Opinions—	210
Salads and Salad Dressing.	39		
Boiled Salad Dressing	40	Soups—	
Fruit Salad	40	Brown Soup Stock	9
		White Soup Stock	9

Sailors' Recipes—

		Tomato Soup	9
		Tomato Broth	10
Dolphin or Bonita	142	Creole Celery Soup	10
To Make Fresh Water "Spin Out" When Supply Is Limited	142	Chicken Cream Tomato Soup	10
Sea Birds	142	Bean Soup	10
Seal Livers and Seal Hearts	142	Tomato Soup	10
Tail of a Shark	142	Cheese Soup	11
Porpoise	143	Cream Potato Soup	11
List of Store Seasonings Sufficient for Twelve Months' Voyage	143	Grapenuts Broth	11
		Tomato	11
		Vegetable	11
Pea Soup	143	Potato	12
Soup and Bouilli	144	Cream of Celery	12
Curried Salt Beef	144	Corn	12
Hot Pot Tom Bowling	144		
Hodge Podge	145	Tables—	184
Beef a la Marine	145		
Peas Pudding	145	Vegetables—	
Plain Suet Pudding	146	Burgess Potatoes	41
Molasses Pudding	146	Stuffed Potatoes	41
Sea Pie	146	Hashed Brown Potatoes	41
Plum Pudding	147	Potato Omelet	41
Yorkshire Pudding	147	Rice Tomatoes	42
Minced Collops	147	Stuffed Tomatoes (Cooked)	42
Sausage Rolls	148	Egyptian Rice	42
Beef Brawn	148	Stuffed Peppers	42
Beef Olives	149	Baked Beans	42
Curried Mutton	149	Baked Beans	43
Scalloped Liver	150	To Can Green Vegetables	43
Rock Cakes	150	Keeping Boiled Corn Hot.	43
Soda Scones	150	Scalloped Sweet Corn	43
Bubble and Squeak	151	Corn Fritters	43
		Beets	44
Sandwiches—		Stewed Cabbage	44
		A Simple Way to Cook Carrots	44
Nut Sandwiches	51	Creamed Celery	44
Water Cress Sandwiches	51	Green Corn Fritters	44

INDEX---Continued

	Page		Page
Vegetarian Department	152	Asparagus Shortcake	124
Nut Roast	123	Curried Rice and Tomatoes	124
Nut Roast with Lentels	123	Biscuit Pates	124
Rice Patties	123	Bananas, Baked and Fried	124
Macaroni Escalloped	123	Delicious Fruit Mixture	124

Made in the USA
San Bernardino, CA
26 February 2020

65026732R00158